IN PRAISE of LEISURE

IN PRAISE of LEISURE

Harold D. Lehman

HERALD PRESS
Scottdale, Pennsylvania
Kitchener, Ontario
1974

Library of Congress Cataloging in Publication Data

Lehman, Harold D.   1921-
  In praise of leisure.

  (The Conrad Grebel lectures, 1973)
  Includes bibliographical references.
  1. Leisure. 2. Work. I. Title. II. Series.
BJ1498.L426   175   74-16399
ISBN 0-8361-1752-2
ISBN 0-8361-1749-2 (pbk.)

IN PRAISE OF LEISURE

Copyright © 1974 by Herald Press, Scottdale, Pa. 15683
Library of Congress Catalog Card Number:
International Standard Book Number: 74-16399
    0-8361-1752-2   (hardcover)
    0-8361-1749-2   (softcover)
Printed in the United States of America

Dedicated to the memory of my father
Daniel W. Lehman
who exemplified in his living
that work and leisure are complementary functions
under the lordship of Christ

CONTENTS

Preface 9
Introduction 13
I. Leisure: Fact and Myth
    1. What Happened to My Leisure? 17
    2. What, Then, Is Leisure? 25
    3. At the Risk of Leisure 38
II. The Age of Leisure
    4. The Advance of Leisure 47
    5. The Retreating Horizon of Man's Response 56
    6. Work and Leisure in the Post-Industrial Age .. 66
III. The Anatomy of Work — The Work Ethic
    7. Work and Its Meanings 77
    8. God's People and Work 85
    9. A Critical Look at the Traditional Work Ethic 97
    10. Christian Vocation, Work, and Job 111
IV. In Praise of Leisure — The Leisure Ethic
    11. God's People and Leisure 123
    12. In Praise of Leisure 133
V. What the New Leisure Says to the Church
    13. The New Leisure — An Opportunity for the Church .. 157
    14. The New Leisure — Implications for the Congregation 174
Notes 185
The Conrad Grebel Lectures 194
Index 196
The Author 200

PREFACE

A French poet once commented, "A poem is never finished; it is abandoned in despair." To revise as long as one can bear it must be a common experience, not only for poets, but also for other writers. This is particularly true when the subject is as encompassing, as current, and as evolving as the social dynamic of leisure. The writer simply articulates his ideas for the time being, realizing that the discussion by its very nature is open-ended and must go on.

For years Christian people maligned leisure as the just dues of the idle derelict or the dubious prerogative of the filthy rich. Horatius Bonar's "Go, labor on, spend and be spent" was given unabashed priority over Phoebe H. Brown's "I love to steal awhile away from ev'ry cumb'ring care." Only a maverick like Henry David Thoreau dared speak of "the days when idleness was the most attractive and productive industry. . . . I was rich, if not in money, in sunny hours and summer days and I spent them lavishly, nor do I regret that I did not waste more of them in the workshop or at the teacher's desk."

A book "in praise of leisure" should accentuate the positive. Indeed this is the design, to recognize leisure as a particular providence of God in our age with great possibilities for personal and social benefit.

Part I of this book recognizes the presence of leisure in Western society. Leisure forces its way upon us for better or for worse. Modern man lives very much at the risk of leisure. It can provide satisfaction and fulfillment; it can bring emptiness and frustration. Leisure can free; it can condemn.

Trends which characterize "the age of leisure" in the last quarter of our century are investigated in Part II. Most of us, farmers included, have a shorter workweek than did our grandparents. We have acquired much of the equipment and many of the gadgets of leisure. Increased affluence and available time have opened up a broad range of leisure pursuits. With it all have come changing societal patterns and individual habits of life.

Since work has been a dominant theme in Western culture, leisure must be viewed as its counterpart. The work ethic influences not only how we think about work but also it predisposes our attitudes about leisure. The meanings of work in our culture, its historical patterns, the emergence of the modern work ethic, and a contemporary Christian view of work are discussed in Part III.

Beginning with the historical patterns of leisure, Part IV attempts to build a Christian ethic of

Preface 11

leisure. Principles are identified from the Scriptures concerning a Christian's use of time. We note the functions which leisure has and search for a distinctly Christian doctrine of leisure. At its best leisure relates to the Christian calling under the lordship of Christ.

In the final section leisure is viewed as complementary to the mission of the church. Leisure brings fresh opportunities, as well as new threats to the church. The congregational program needs to make adjustments as it seeks to perform its ministry in the new leisure era. It may well be that in the new leisure the congregation will find exciting new possibilities of fellowship, service, and worship.

And now, in acknowledging those who assisted in the venture of this book, my thanks go first to the Conrad Grebel Lectureship Committee for inviting me to this assignment. It proved to be not only an exercise in research and writing but more importantly an experience of commitment to the essence of leisure — an attitude of freedom and sense of calm. My idols of busyness, of gadgets, and even of leisure pursuits have taken on lesser priority. The ideal of leisure at its highest remains for me a continuing goal.

To the mentors who read and offered helpful criticisms on the manuscript, I express appreciation. This committee consisted of Helen Alderfer, John A. Lapp, and Tilman R. Smith. The typist, Sara Ann Showalter, deserves thanks for a job neatly done. Paul M. Schrock provided the technical assistance necessary at the publishing end of the project.

Highest recognition is reserved for my family. Even though family leisure during this period suffered curtailment, they were patient and supportive. Son Dan, as an unemployed college student in the summer before his senior year, was actively interested in the project. He researched and wrote Part II of the book. Ruth, my wife, as ever loyal supporter and discerning critic, assisted immeasurably every step of the way.

Finally to those of you who listened to the lectures at the colleges and seminaries or in congregations, I express appreciation for your interest and helpful feedback. It was in this kind of exchange that the issues of leisure came most clearly into focus.

Harold D. Lehman
August 18, 1973

INTRODUCTION

The question of leisure has been a concern of thoughtful persons throughout history. In ancient times leisure was the basis of what was called civilized life. The leisured classes produced the arts, literature, and philosophy which we continue to admire.

For modern North America leisure has become a perplexing problem both in terms of quantity and quality. Whether moderns have more free time than their ancestors is not yet apparent. It is clear that the average worker puts fewer hours on the job. But in turn workers spend more time getting to work, repairing appliances, and keeping appointments for their children.

The issue is how one uses leisure time. Jacques Ellul in *The Technological Society* scrutinizes the "psychological dissociation between intelligence and action which our technical society tends to produce." He laments those persons who express their lives in either work or leisure but not in both. "It is impossible," he says, "to fragment man's personality without weakening it."

It is the genius of Harold Lehman's study of leisure to find the proper expression of work and leisure in the context of Christian vocation:

> A Christian considers his leisure not as an end in itself, nor as the opposite of work, but as a function in his life which contributes to his calling. He views rest, relaxation, fun, and activity in light of how they enhance or detract from this vocation.

Throughout the book Lehman emphasizes this theme of seeing life as a unit, a rhythm of work and leisure, both of which are filled with purpose. Not only does he deal with the theological and philosophical issue of leisure but he provides an ethical framework for planning and evaluating the experience of leisure.

The Conrad Grebel Lectureship Committee [see page 194] is grateful for this solid, readable contribution to the teaching ministry of the church.

John A. Lapp, Dean
Goshen College
July 23, 1973

I. Leisure: Fact and Myth

1. *What Happened to My Leisure?*

The real problem of your leisure is to keep other people from using it. — *Lindsay Post*

"Name it and you will destroy it." This intriguing riddle sticks in my mind from those childhood days when it was fun to ask and try to solve such puzzlers. The answer to this one, "Silence," simply added to the mystery. How can something be identified and by that same act its destruction be decreed? How can something both exist and not exist at the same time?

This is the paradox of leisure in American society. We have it and yet it somehow evades us. While it is estimated that the labor-saving devices in the typical household perform the toil of ninety servants, we feel as busy as ever. Within the past century the average workweek has tumbled from seventy hours to below forty hours. Even so, we find scarcely more time to do the things we like than did our grandparents.

We work hard in anticipation of leisure but find it as illusive as the pot of gold at the end of the rainbow.

Leisure is both fact and myth. Although our times have been variously described as the age of leisure, the leisure revolution, the mass leisure, or the leisure society, its realization has not lived up to its promise. On a personal basis the question, "What shall I do with my leisure time?" is more appropriately stated by many of us, "What happened to my leisure; where did it go?" Some simply ponder, "How can I latch on to some of it?"

What happened to my leisure? Case One

"Virginia Family Plight: $14,365 a Year and No Fun." This recent *Washington Post* headline introduced an article about a young suburban couple. With their three small children the family lives in a new house just recently purchased. By all appearances and the common yardsticks they are living well. They own a new Chevrolet, a houseful of furniture, a console color TV, and a second car — an eight-year-old Chrysler.

The husband, a computer operator for the Census Bureau, works in nearby Maryland. His regular salary combined with overtime pay earned over the weekends was $14,365 in 1972. His free time at home is reduced further because he must commute sixty-four miles round trip to his work.

Unfortunately, the realities of keeping up their standard of living tend to deprive the family of the opportunity to enjoy leisure time. Last year they spent $2,000 more than they earned mainly because of buying too much on credit cards. Two years ago they purchased a camper but they haven't found time to use it yet. Because of weekend overtime work there are no blocks of time available for vacation. Besides, they don't have the ready cash for an extended time off. Ironically, just to store their camper costs one hundred dollars each year. They daydream about a trip to Florida, or to the Pennsylvania Dutch Country, or camping on the New Jersey beaches, but so far it hasn't happened.

An economist commenting on this family situation declares it to be another example of the myth of the leisured class. Although this family is living well, its position is precarious because of heavy indebtedness. It really is run to death maintaining the American standard of a good life. There is little time for leisure. Such is the plight of $14,365 a year and no fun! [1]

While this instance is by no means an isolated one, it may help to bring the complexities of leisure closer home to portray another case — a hypothetical yet typical family. A sample week's schedule shows how immediately apparent and frustrating the problems of family leisure can be.

What happened to my leisure? Case Two

Father's work in the office keeps him going from 8:30 to 4:30 each day plus many evenings when he brings work home in his attache case. Monday nights are reserved for school board meetings and other committee work. On Wednesday there is a midweek service at the church; Friday there is choir practice. After the game of golf on Saturday morning, the rest of the day is usually occupied with repair and lawn work around the house.

Mother has a clerking job in a department store three days a week plus two evenings, Wednesdays and Fridays. Her ladies' fellowship group from the church meets Tuesday evenings. Thursday evenings are reserved for shopping, and the rest of the time is used for caring for the family, meal preparation, washing, ironing, and cleaning.

Tom, the teenager, has varsity basketball practice three times a week after school and games on Friday evenings. His youth group meets at the church Wednesday evenings. On Saturdays he bags groceries at the local supermarket. Jane, his younger sister, is a Girl Scout, takes a weekly piano lesson, has an occasional slumber party at home or at a friend's house, and spends most evenings on schoolwork.

Sunday, a kind of togetherness day for the family, finds them attending church and Sunday school and enjoying the family dinner afterward. But then varied interests take over again. Mother prefers to visit neighbors, Father reads, Tom watches football on TV, and Jane hikes or bicycles with friends. Depending upon what is scheduled on the evening program at church, the family may attend. More often they do not.

Somehow the family interests grow more diverse each year. Any occasion to include the four together in some leisure activity must be planned well ahead. Fortunately, they have been able to have a vacation trip each summer and a few weekend jaunts during the school season. Otherwise their family leisure is plagued by schedule conflicts and varied interests. They talk about this problem sometimes, but haven't arrived at any solutions yet.

What happened to my leisure? Some clues

Throughout history man's waking hours have been occupied with work. Against this background of work, leisure has developed. Even though man has always lived by toil, it is only in modern times that his work has been productive enough to yield him substantial free time. Leisure, it turns out, happens to be an unprepared-for by-product of work.

While leisure historically was the privilege of a small upper class, it has now become the possession of nearly everyone. The "leisure class" has yielded to the new phenomenon of "mass leisure." Ironically it is in the hard-working industrialized societies that leisure comes to the fore and thus confronts its creators with its baffling problems. James A. Garfield said over one hundred years ago that "we may divide the whole struggle of the human race into two chapters: first, the fight to get leisure; second, what shall we do with our leisure when we get it?" [2] To these questions we now add the one under present consideration, "What happened to our leisure?"

Failure to accept leisure for its own values

One clue to the illusiveness of leisure is that we tend to separate work and leisure into warring opposites rather than to accept their complementary functions in our lives. We find it difficult to accept leisure for its own sake. Rather, we judge it on the basis of work values, carrying into our leisure time the same aggressiveness and drive for productivity. Consequently, we miss leisure's contributions and thus wonder what happened to our leisure time.

C. Wright Mills in his book on the American middle classes catches this competitive work-leisure attitude. He maintains that work and leisure have now come to a sharp, almost absolute break from each other.[3] Time on the job and time at leisure are well-defined segments in a man's schedule and tend not to overlap each other. This is particularly true if a man's work is a boring grind and of little real significance. For him leisure becomes a welcome escape, a time that he can pull himself together again with some pleasurable activity. "The cycle of work and leisure gives rise to two quite different images of self: the everyday image based upon work, and the holiday image, based upon leisure."[4]

This distinction between time spent at work and time spent in leisure is also evident by the verbs we commonly attach to both activities. As Max Kaplan points out, "In work one 'sells' time or 'uses' it; in play one 'spends' time, 'kills' it, 'enjoys' it or 'wastes' it. For each we have separate clothes, hours, companions or colleagues, status positions, places, automobiles, and even languages."[5]

Intrusion of other nonwork activities

Another competitor of our leisure is the time demanded by nonjob obligations. Home duties and the activities involved in our nonwork associations make serious intrusions on leisure time. The real culprits are such activities as committee meetings, appointments, and obligations which we take upon ourselves. While these may yield leisure benefits they are more often regarded as duties. Consequently their effect is more in conflict with leisure rather than in support of it.

Time demands made by the consumer economy

A third clue to the disappearance of leisure time lies in the fact that the consumption of goods produced during work time puts heavy demands upon one's leisure time. Like Emerson, who noted that if he kept a cow "the cow would milk him," the acquiring and use of possessions may take away from the possessor more than they give. Swedish economist, Staffan B. Linder, in a recent book, *The Harried Leisure Class*, says that when economic productivity increases leisure time decreases correspondingly.[6] The use, enjoyment, care, and maintenance of all the commodities we produce demand an ever-increasing proportion of time. We acquire bigger houses and more appliances to keep up, larger lawns to take care of, a swimming pool to maintain, and a television set to repair. These numerous conveniences and even leisure equipment not only claim work time to acquire in the first place but now demand time for their use and servicing.

Since time is a nonexpandable resource, the focus must be on how this supply of time is used. While we may conceivably buy more of everything, we cannot do more of everything. People commonly make the mistake of acquiring more articles than they have time to use. Linder warns that as consumption time in the future continues to rise, our cultural progress will suffer decline. Cultivation of the mind and spirit, while they may demand little in material goods, do require the factor of time. Unfortunately, it is this kind of time which stands to suffer most from the intrusions of a consumer economy. [7]

We are also aware that the volume and quality of services, both private and public, have not been able to keep pace with the increase of goods. For instance, it takes more time and effort to get someone to take care of a minor repair job around the house. The postal system illustrates the difficulty which a service has in attempting to keep up to the demands placed upon it. Even in the areas of personal care and maintenance Linder notes a tendency to rob ourselves. Some people regard sleep as a waste of time and thus try to cut down the number of hours needed. Cooking, eating, and exercise are all time-consuming activities which we tend to short-cut for the sake of saving time. A widely advertised book, *How to Raise Children at Home in Your Spare Time*, suggests that we even approve the reduction of another traditional maintenance task, that of child-raising. [8]

These several clues serve to illustrate why leisure time seems to decrease, despite the news that we should have more free time. While the reality of Linder's thesis of the harried leisure class is one which most of us know too well by experience, there are possibilities for reorienting values and reordering time priorities. We turn next, however, to investigating further the complexities of leisure and how it relates to such concepts as recreation, play, work, and time.

2. What, Then, Is Leisure?

Leisure is the best of all possessions. — *Socrates*

Leisure is a weasel word — hard to pin down. Like the comments of the blind men who each described the elephant in terms of his own limited contact, the definitions of leisure vary depending upon the elements suggested. Each adds something to the understanding of the word but none is complete in itself. Being a culturally attached word, leisure has meanings which vary according to person, era of time, or society involved.

Max Kaplan, director for the Center for Studies of Leisure at the University of South Florida, summarizes the complexity of leisure as follows:

> At one time it [leisure] deals with the momentary fragment of life: someone sits quietly and knits, another reads, a third listens to a symphony or records, a fourth drives his family into the countryside to celebrate a New England fall day. At the same time the subject of leisure is as magnificent in its dimensions as the institutions

and values of the culture or the milieu: the matter of loneliness, the nature of audiences, and the meaning of mass media, the roots of family life, the perception of time, the uses of technology, the psychological-economic dimensions of the guaranteed annual income, the symbols of social class, the motivations and satisfactions in work. What is momentary and private is not unimportant, and what is of grand design to social inquiry is not impractical. We must, in this field, deal with many realities and many disguises; the pragmatic and the symbolic, the committed and the parasitic, the spurious and the authentic. [1]

In common usage *leisure* generally has one of three meanings. It may refer to a block of time (time left over from work), an activity (a recreational or play function), or an attitude (a spirit of release and freedom). The context in which the word appears usually makes its usage quite clear. A progression is suggested by the three ways of defining the term: leisure as time is the most elementary, while leisure as attitude is the most difficult to experience.

Leisure as antithesis to work

"Leisure is time free from required work when a person may rest, amuse himself, and do the things he likes to do." [2] This dictionary definition considers work to be man's real responsibility and leisure to be free-from-work time. It implies that leisure is primarily a rest or diversion and in effect prepares one for more work.

This definition, while being the conventional notion about leisure, is misleading by itself. It makes opposites of work and leisure and infers that they are competitive blocks of time with differing values. Leisure is more than servant to work.

Leisure as paramount activity of man

In the classical Greek view leisure stood as a high privilege of man. Aristotle thought that the aim of education was the wise use of leisure. The Greeks tended to equate leisure with contemplative and intellectual pursuits. They would not have understood our highly work-oriented way of life. To them, true happiness appeared in leisure. The capacity to use leisure rightly lay at the basis of the free man's whole life; everything else, work included, found its meaning in relation to leisure. The ordinary toils of life were simply a form of nonleisure.

Despite the idealism of the classical view, it had several limitations. It made leisure an exclusive prerogative of the elite or ruling class and denied the possibility of leisure's universal application. In limiting leisure to activity of the mind it failed to recognize the leisure values of a wider range of physical activities.

Leisure as activity for its own sake

Leisure is an activity performed for its own sake or as its own end. Sebastian De Grazia, a chief proponent of this view, explains:

> What a man does when he does not have to do anything, he does for its own sake, but he does not think of it as fun or having a good time. It may be difficult or easy, pleasant or unpleasant, and look suspiciously

like hard work, but it is something he wants to do. That is all. [3]

This is a rather difficult concept to understand because we commonly justify the things we do, particularly leisure-time activities, in terms of something else. A high respect for the importance of work makes us uncomfortable in engaging in any activity which does not have utilitarian values either directly or remotely. Leisure for its own sake seems like a waste of time. Walter Kerr in *The Decline of Pleasure* pointedly illustrates the American hang-up about utilitarian leisure:

> We are all of us compelled to read for profit, party for contacts, lunch for contracts, bowl for unity, drive for mileage, gamble for charity, go out for the evening for the greater glory of the municipality, and stay home for the weekend to rebuild the house. [4]

Leisure as freedom

Our word leisure is derived from the Latin word *licere,* meaning "to be permitted, to be free." Freedom is an important clue to the meaning of leisure. Externally this freedom means release from work and necessity; internally, from boredom and apathy. There are many things which a person may do in his free time but only those activities qualify in which there is choice and the absence of compulsion.

While freedom is an important characteristic of leisure, this definition does not imply that freedom and leisure are synonymous. It is possible to find freedom in work as well as in leisure. Ideally, all of a Christian's time is free under God and we live in responsibility for how we use that freedom in all that we do.

Leisure as attitude of mind and condition of spirit
Leisure is a quality of life, not to be locked in with quantitative measures of time, work, or activity. It demands a disengagement from material concepts and may be experienced anytime, even at work. Work and leisure, at their best, converge into an attitude and spirit in which they can no longer be distinguished. It was in this vein that Thomas Edison could remark that he never did a day's work in his life.

In his book *Religion and Leisure in America* Robert Lee says, "Leisure is the growing time of the spirit. Leisure provides the occasion for learning and freedom, for growth and expression, for rest and restoration, for rediscovering life in its entirety."[5] Josef Pieper, the Swiss Catholic philosopher, discusses leisure as a mental and spiritual attitude characterized by a sense of calm, of letting things happen, of serenity, of contemplative celebration, and of reaching out for wholeness. This level of leisure is a high ideal.[6]

Leisure: summary statements
Two authorities in the leisure field have attempted definitions which summarize the basic elements in leisure. One is given by Joffre Dumazedier in the "Leisure" article in the *International Encyclopedia of the Social Sciences*. He reduces the basic characteristics of leisure into two categories. First, there is "the absence of certain social obligations." Leisure provides freedom from the usual responsibilities of work, family,

society, or religion. It has a certain character of disinterestedness because it is not governed by utilitarian, commercial, or ideological purposes.

Second, there is the "presence of certain qualities of personal fulfillment." As an end in itself, leisure provides for the satisfaction of individual needs. It can open up a world of self-transcendence characterized by joyful feelings of freedom, fulfillment, and significance.[7]

Another more definitive statement on leisure was given by Max Kaplan at the National Conference on Social Welfare at Dallas, Texas, in 1971.

> Leisure, then, can be said to consist of relatively self-determined activities and experiences that fall into one's economically free-time roles, that are seen as leisure by participants, that are psychologically pleasant in anticipation and recollection, that potentially cover the whole range of commitment and intensity, that contain characteristic norms and restraints, and provide opportunities for recreation, personal growth, and service to others.[8]

Recreation, the accepted use of leisure

Recreation is commonly referred to as the wholesome use of leisure time. Since its meaning is so closely tied to leisure, the term is subject to all the variations noted under the leisure definitions. Thus, recreation may be referred to as a diversion from work, as an area of abundant living, as an activity for its own sake, as an attitude or spirit, or as a time of choice. One distinctive element suggested is that recreation should re-create, restore, and refresh the participant. While renewal is an ideal in recreation, it

What, Then, Is Leisure? 31

is recognized that if free choice is present persons may use their leisure in a wide range of ways from the socially acceptable and useful to the harmful and even destructive.

Recreation involves activity of one kind or another. It may be the rigorous activity of playing tennis or ice skating or the mental and emotional effort of reading a book or listening to music. Because the recreational needs, interests, and wishes of people differ, recreation takes many forms. One man's recreation may be another man's drudgery. Cultivating a garden may be a splendid form of recreation for the man with a desk job. To his teenager, however, the same activity is a chore. Or an activity may be a pleasure at one time under certain circumstances, but may elicit boredom in another setting. One's attitude toward an activity is a decisive factor in whether or not it has recreational value. If the motive is enjoyment and personal satisfaction and the doing of it has its own appeal, it is recreation.

Play, a function of leisure

Play, a related word of great versatility, is more easily described than defined. In everyday experience we often observe the play of children and youth. We are aware of the intense play activities among the young of many species of animal life. Generally we find it easy to differentiate play from work.

Tom Sawyer, you will recall, felt his anticipated day of play was ruined by Aunt Polly's decree to whitewash the fence. Our sympathies continue with Tom when Ben Rogers, the neighborhood bully, comes into sight impersonating the *Big Missouri* and taunts him, "Hi yi. You're up a stump, ain't you. . . . You got to work, hey?"[9] It's with a sense of comic relief that we watch Tom maneuver Ben into begging for the privilege of doing his work for him.

Many thinkers have attempted to analyze play, its basic elements, and its meanings to the participant. Among these was the Dutch scholar, Johann Huizinga, who regarded the instinct of play as the source of civilization. He identified the essential characteristics of play in the following definition:

> . . . we might call it a free activity standing quite consciously outside "ordinary" life as being "not serious," but at the same time absorbing the player intensely and utterly. It is an activity connected with no material interest, and no profit can be gained by it. It proceeds within its own proper boundaries of time and space according to fixed rules and in an orderly manner. It promotes the formation of social groupings which tend to surround themselves with secrecy and to stress the difference from the common world by disguise or other means.[10]

All ages of humans play, whether child or adult, although the play of adults is often referred to as recreation. Thus play may be considered as a function of leisure. Play activity usually occurs in some kind of social setting which has its own structure, rules, and sanctions. Rules give to play a sense of fairness and are a regulatory device. In the more complex forms of game activity the absence of such rules and sanctions would be chaotic. With its own boundaries of time and place, even the young child knows when an activity is play and when it is not play.

As with leisure, play activity is characterized by freedom and spontaneity. Play is essentially an end in itself. To the participant it is real activity, one in which he can become completely involved. It possesses the qualities of enjoyment, fun, and happiness and is free from the anxieties and burdens associated with work.

As a meaningful activity within itself play serves as a means of self-expression, mutual enjoyment, and release from tension or loneliness. Play tends to involve the total personality, body and soul, and supplies satisfactions not found in work. It provides that necessary change and diversion from the routine and monotony of life. Like leisure, play has within it the powers both to free or to enslave the human spirit.[11]

Of work and technology

Sixty years ago Richard C. Cabot, [12] a Christian medical professor at Harvard University, stated in his book *What Men Live By* that life is made up of four important dimensions: work, play, love, and worship. An overbalance of any one of these to the exclusion of another results in a distorted Christian personality. Cabot's thesis is still sound. As one of these areas, work refers to the physical and mental effort by which man makes a livelihood. It is the endeavor expended to provide the physical necessities of life — food, clothing, and shelter — as well as to provide a whole range of things we need and desire. Work has many inducements, accomplishments, and satisfactions both from within and without. In proper perspective work carries with it the fulfillment of purpose and usefulness.

While work was accomplished traditionally by manual labor, it has now been taken over largely by technology. By technology is meant "the totality of hand and machine tools plus the full range of intellectual tools which men make and use to make and do things with."[13]

The aim of technology, at least of a technological society, is to provide man with all the commodities he desires. In the process, technology has been able to replace work in the traditional sense. Modern production is far more the result of mechanical and industrial inventions than of physical labor. Technology has a direct relationship to leisure in that its effect is to free man from his boring menial tasks and perhaps someday to free him from the necessity of working at all.

Since leisure is referred to as one of the uses of *time*, this too is a concept to consider. Time is a gift from God. While time is commonly thought of chronologically in terms of temporal duration, its truest meaning lies in the quality of content which fills it. How we spend our time affects the nature of that time.

Cyclical view of time

Time can be measured in relation to cycles of a single day, a week, month, year, decade, century, or millennium. Time repeats itself and is marked by the reoccurrence of events: the rising and setting of the sun, the rhythm of the seasons, the circuit of growth and decay. According to this view one cannot speak of wasting time because time that has passed is not really lost; it will come again. Neither is time cumulative; the future will be much like the past. In fact, this particular way of looking at time lends itself to an inherently leisurely philosophy of life.

> To every thing there is a season, and a time to every purpose under the heaven: a time to be born, and a time to die; a time to plant, and a time to pluck up that which is planted; a time to kill, and a time to heal; a time to break down, and a time to build up....[14]

Without doing violence to these thoughts, we might add, "A time for work and a time for leisure."

Linear view of time

Time can also be thought of in linear fashion, a progression toward an end or goal. Time has direction, a teleology, a culmination toward which it moves. As children of God we stand at a particular point on this time line, recognizing that we share in this ongoing procession of God and His people. This lays upon us a serious responsibility because time is precious, a resource with great potential. It can be "redeemed" or it can be squandered and lost forever. How we use it is important because time will not pass this way again.

Linear time also lends itself to the optimistic outlook; there is always the hope of a better day tomorrow. In the biblical view time will culminate in the great parousia when Christ will fully reign as King of kings and Lord of lords and time shall be no more.

Qualitative view of time

A third view of time and a dominant biblical view emphasizes its qualitative character. Time's truest measure is its content or eventfulness, particularly as it reflects God's actions in the affairs of men. Time is in God's hands. Robert Lee[15] speaks of this as "realistic" or existential time, the time of opportunity and fulfillment.

The content of time is endowed by God; its fulfillment is man's opportunity. When Christ under the appointment of God began His first preaching mission in Galilee He proclaimed. "The time is fulfilled."[16] Our time is important because God has chosen to act in human history in our behalf.

Of time and leisure

The precise measurement of time is a rather recent accomplishment. While some of the famous town clocks in European cities are centuries old, it is only since the mass production of timepieces in the last century that it has been possible to regulate man's activities so exactly. Now we sleep, wake up, eat, work, play, and worship by the clock. In short, time is master of our lives. Failure to order one's life by the clock in Western culture can be disastrous. Clock time, as the regulator of human activity, has become the unit by which we consciously measure work and leisure. It is a short step then to equate time and money since time spent at work results in tangible coin. With the money earned by time man can buy leisure, at least the gadgets of leisure. The only thing he cannot buy is more time.

From a quantitative viewpoint De Grazia divides man's activities into four time categories. First there is the time spent at work, the 40-hour week, plus time spent by the multiple jobholder in moonlighting. A second category is work-related time. Commuting to and from work and the activities in preparation for one's work may take considerable time. In the third place, subsistence time includes that necessary for sleeping and eating, shopping and cooking, and personal and home maintenance. Finally there is free time, the time remaining in the 24 hours each day after the other three activities are attended to. Obviously there is overlapping in these segments of time. The motive behind the activity may determine in which category it will fall.[17]

3. At the Risk of Leisure

A society is what it does in its free time — August Heckscher

What would you do with leisure? Dr. Jay B. Nash, a foremost American philosopher on recreation and leisure, once asked one thousand adults what they would do with a year off. His question was stated thus: "Beginning tomorrow morning you are given a full year, fully financed, with your family cared for, to do something you have always wanted to do. What do you choose?"[1]

How would you answer? Would you travel, write a novel, paint a picture, hunt or fish, take a service assignment, go back to college, learn to play the violin, mountain-climb or ski?

In analyzing his replies Dr. Nash found that most individuals indicated an activity which was already one of their interests or hobbies. A year off would simply provide time to pursue the activity to a fuller extent. Furthermore, he noted that most of the activities chosen were those in which the person had acquired an interest before the age of 21. A year off would give the person an opportunity to do something he had always wanted to do but hadn't fully accomplished because of limitations of time, finance, or opportunity.

It seems that specific leisure interests are acquired at an early age and that in adulthood we seldom expand our leisure interests or develop new leisure skills. This does not mean that we can't learn new things after thirty, but that there's a tendency not to branch out into new experiences. Dr. Nash suggests that a good way to keep youthful is to develop one new skill every year. Learn to type, to play the piano, to crochet, to swim, to knit, to construct birdhouses, or to accomplish any kind of skill which you do not have at present. This is a sure cure for fossilizing before one's time.

This study also inquired where people had first learned their leisure interests and skills. Seventy percent had begun the activity in the home; parents were the teachers in 44 percent of the cases. Leisure interests seem to be established at an early age and are strongly influenced by the home and parents.

Probably the most important point to be gained from Dr. Nash is that his proposition about a year off to pursue leisure interests is not really a hypothetical one. We do, indeed, have time off for leisure pursuits. It may not come in the form of a sabbatical year but it does come in terms of our margin of free time. How to use these segments of time is our responsibility. What ought we do? Can we be trusted with leisure? Dare we accept leisure? Are we willing to assume the risks of leisure?

Unfortunately, history offers us little help for answering these questions. In one instance we recall the downfall of the ancient Greeks and Romans who misused their leisure, corrupting their societies through excesses in spectator sports and sensual debauchery. In another instance we remember that leisure has never been quite respectable in our own American past. Historically, it has been associated with a sense of frustration and guilt rather than with the experience of release and wholeness.

But now leisure has arrived. Its presence is no longer an option. How is leisure to be used? Can leisure yield constructive benefits to the glory of God or does it condemn us to emptiness, hedonism, and self-indulgence? Is leisure, in fact, a blessing or a curse?

At the risk of leisure

Jay B. Nash reminds us that leisure has potential in both directions. Using a simple diagram (*next page*) he illustrates how leisure can apply itself to a wide range of values from those expressed in destructive acts of delinquency and crime to the positive expressions of the highest in creative activity.

In terms of quality man uses his leisure time in a wide variety of ways. Below the "zero line" Dr. Nash places all the unsocial and antisocial deeds of human delinquency. Some of these are acts against oneself; others are acts against society. In either case they are

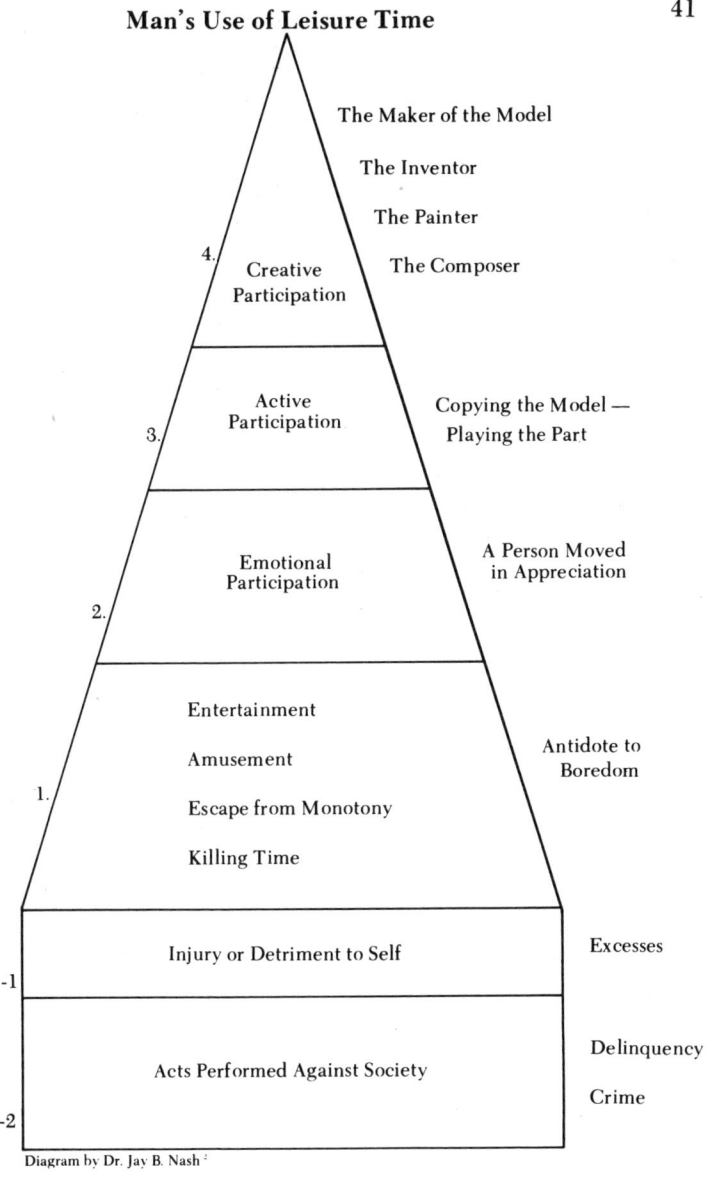

Diagram by Dr. Jay B. Nash

destructive of human values and represent a negative use of leisure.

Passive participation
Beginning at the base line of the triangle, the first level is that of passive participation. Low on this scale is the aimless "killing of time," with nothing attempted and therefore nothing achieved excepting the inevitable passing of time. Here also are located the various forms of passive spectator involvement. At their lowest level they represent simply an escape from boredom. One can get away from reality at least for a time but when the merry-go-round stops, reality is still there. Amusement and entertainment represent higher forms in this category.

While it is true that there is some value in spectator activity, it does not follow necessarily that the more "spectatoritis" the better. Watching an athletic event, even though it may be largely passive, can be a good diversion from the pressures of daily life. Other recreational activities, for instance watching television, demand or deserve little active response. In any case, Nash warns us to be master of the situation rather than to allow ourselves to be captivated by that which merely amuses or entertains. The whole point of his argument is that leisure at its best involves some sort of active participation.

Emotional participation
Proceeding to the next higher category in the Nash diagram one may participate emotionally in an experience or in the creative work of another. When

someone touches your inner feelings or ties in with some meaningful experience you feel an emotional response. When others perform for your benefit through music, art, literature, drama, or other expressive arts, their creative work draws from you some appreciative reaction. You participate at the emotional level. We all know something of the leisure-time satisfaction which comes with a feeling response to the breathless quiet of a Vermeer, the majestic building swell of Bach, or the all-encompassing rhythmic vision of Dante.

Active participation
Above the level of emotional response comes the actual participation of the one who plays the part or copies the model. The actor on the stage, the athlete on the playing floor, the singer in the choral group, or the seamstress sewing from the pattern are all actively involved. Their participation is quite different from that of the mere onlooker or even the one emotionally moved by a production. This is the level where most of us perform recreationally as active participants whether it be in art, music, sports, or crafts. We simply utilize the models handed to us by the creator in the field and obtain leisure benefits in reproducing or copying their models to the best of our abilities.

Creative participation
At the apex of the leisure triangle stands the crowning activity, the creative acts of man. Here an original art model is constructed, the score of a new symphony is composed, an innovative idea takes form

as a mechanical invention, or the poet's creative expressions are recorded on paper. In any case a new construct has been created. This represents the highest quality of leisure activity and as such stands close to the benefits and satisfactions to be derived from work at its highest. Any master in the art of living draws no sharp distinctions between his work and leisure at their creative best. The satisfactions to be derived from creativity in work and leisure are ultimately identical.[3]

In summary, modern man lives very much at the risk of leisure. It has been forced upon us for better or for worse. Leisure can build; it can destroy. It can provide satisfaction and fulfillment; it can bring emptiness and frustration. Leisure can be fun; it can bore us. Leisure can free; it can condemn.

II. The Age of Leisure

4. The Advance of Leisure

The leisure which the atomic age will bring may make peace more horrible than war. We face the dreadful prospect of hour after hour, even day after day, with nothing to do. After we have read all the comic books, traveled all the miles, seen all the movies, what shall we do then?

— Robert Hutchins

The rash of concern over the concept of man's leisure is a recent phenomenon. The radical change from overwork to overleisure marks a shifting focus from an age of toil and labor to an age of free time. Hutchins' statement could not have been made one hundred years ago. Then only a select few enjoyed extensive leisure; certainly no one worried about an overabundance of free time.

Although the discussion of leisure has gained increasing importance among thinkers in recent decades, there is by no means agreement as to what constitutes leisure or in fact whether the age of leisure is really approaching at all. This chapter will look at the problem, sift through the controversy, and examine the fact of leisure in the last quarter of this century.

At first glance it is obvious that leisure is increasing. Industrialism and automation, spiraling production capacity, longer periods of pre-work education, extended life-spans with more retirement years, more holidays and vacations, all point to the fact of increased leisure and free time. Some economists and sociologists even point to an inevitable cybernated Utopia of the future.

Yet all around us, men seem unceasingly busy. More people are on the highways going faster and farther. More workers crowd the cities each morning as they push their way toward their jobs. More money is earned; more money is spent; presumably more money is wasted. Are these the symptoms of a dream world of leisure-time happiness?

Educator and Poet Geoffrey Godby[2] in an article entitled, "Leisure: Nearing the Receding Horizon," coined in this title an apt phrase for our madly busy "Age of Leisure." Special attention will be given in this section to the two phases of his statement: first, advancing leisure or the causes of the new leisure potential, and second, the retreating horizon or man's response to this potential. Last, we shall present what it will be like to live in a world of great leisure potential — who will have the leisure and how will it be used?

Any study of leisure-time potential is necessarily limited to subjective evaluations. For example, it is difficult to set a boundary between leisure and enjoyable work on the one hand or leisure and boring inactivity on the other. Even when a precise working definition of leisure is agreed upon, accurate compilation of data is extremely complex. Nevertheless, work-force statistics, time-budget studies, production rates, recreational participation records, and other clues do hold the key to at least semiaccurate quantitative measurements of leisure.

Increased production due to cybernation

Perhaps the foremost factor affecting the amount of leisure potential in any society is the industrial stage of that society. The productivity of its labor force determines the extent of nonworking time or leisure potential that it can support. The modern industrial worker produces six times more goods every hour than did his grandfather. The farm worker of 1900 produced enough fiber and food for eight people. During the mid 1960s he could supply the needs of twenty-five consumers.[3]

Most of this spiraling production can be attributed to the increased utilization of cybernation. Cybernation is a term coined to describe the combination of machine muscle or automation and machine thought or cybernetics. If cybernation reduces by one half the time required for a worker to produce a breadbox, one of several alternatives will result. Either the factory must convince the world that it needs twice as many breadboxes, or one half of the laborers must be laid off, or it must develop a new product and a corresponding desire for that product.

Our nation is faced with such a choice according to a Department of Health, Education, and Welfare research report. By 1985 we must sustain either an 80 percent rise in per capita gross national product or a similarly impressive rise in leisure time. If our production remains constant, cybernation will give us a choice between a 22-hour workweek, a 27-hour work year, or a 38-year-old retirement age, or some other leisure-time alternative. The report predicts that two thirds of the advances made by cybernation result in increased production or the formation of new kinds of jobs, one third in increased leisure.[4]

The increased leisure alternative is not always pleasant. While automation creates new kinds of jobs, it also tends to displace existing kinds of work. The United States Secretary of Labor estimated that automation dries up two million jobs every year. For example, 130,000 telephone operators were employed in 1950. Ten years later employment had fallen by nearly 40 percent. In another popular semi-skilled job, that of machine bookkeeping, hiring stopped altogether during the mid 1960s in New York City.[5]

Shortening of the workweek

New leisure potential may affect both established work patterns and off-the-job free-time potential. Perhaps the most spectacular change concerning on-the-job patterns during the past one hundred years is the length of the workweek. According to Max Kaplan the average workweek in 1850 was 72 hours. By 1900 only 60 hours per week were spent on the job and forty years later work time was down to 44 hours per week. Now labor time has dipped to slightly under forty hours.[6] An increasing trend is developing toward

The Advance of Leisure

a four-day workweek with a three-day weekend.

Several years ago two systems analysts, Herman Kahn and Anthony J. Wiener, collaborated on a systematic projection of the year 2000 based on all available data and trends since 1900. Their work was exhaustive and included several tables and sections concerning the state of leisure time in the year 2000. They projected that by the end of the century work time could fall to a 28-hour week with a 13-week vacation every year. Thus, the American work year would be reduced to 984 hours[7] as compared to its current length of 1976 hours.[8]

The story behind these figures is a staggering example of rapid change. If we accept Kaplan's statistics of a 35-hour reduction in work time per week in the past 120 years we find that with every decade, the average weekly work time has been reduced by three hours. The steelworker whose grandfather labored for six long twelve-hour days every week now works no more than five eight-hour shifts.

Lengthened vacations and holidays

Increased vacation time marks another major leisure advance for labor during the past century. A worker could once only expect extra free days on a few legal holidays and religious celebrations. Vacation time has now blossomed to a full sixteen days every year.[9] Labor seems to place an even higher priority on block free time than on workweek reduction.

Long-term vacations for the average worker may be imminent. Kahn and Wiener's economic scenarios for the leisure-oriented society of AD 2000 predict three-day weekends plus a thirteen-week yearly vacation which, added to the ten legal holidays, gives 218 days off every year as compared to only 147 on the job.[10] It seems quite clear that labor patterns are changing rapidly enough to make avocation rather than vocation man's number one concern for the last quarter of the twentieth century.

But, surprisingly, the leisure revolution does not end with new workweek and vacation-time innovations. Marked trends in off-the-job developments also fan the flames of free-time potential. Not only does the laborer work less every week and every year, but he is likely also to have more years to spend outside the work force.

Extended period of education

One factor in the growth of nonwork time concerns the postponement of work by young people.[11] From the years 1950-1963 labor participation in the age 14-19 bracket dropped 15.5 percent. Most of this change came as a result of the increased importance of post-high school education. Presently a youth's vocation may be postponed some ten years after puberty, whereas a century ago the young began to work as soon as and sometimes before they were physically capable of holding a job. Although irate parents sometimes quote these figures as proof of the permissively reared, lazy younger generation, the simple fact remains that cybernation has dried up many unskilled or semiskilled positions. Therefore, many youth find themselves lacking job opportunities. Education is one alternative that insures a relatively stable future.

Earlier retirement and longer life-span

The trend toward earlier retirement is an important social dynamic of our times. An illustration of this movement is a 1970 agreement between the United Automobile Workers and the auto companies known as "30 and Out." After thirty years on the job this plan permits the worker to retire with a lifetime pension.

Not only do people want "out" at a younger age but also the companies and labor unions see earlier retirements as being in their best interests in order to spread the work around and open up jobs for younger persons. Congress is pressured to lower the age of Social Security benefits and to make retirement more desirable. While this early retirement ethic can be debated, it seems to be the direction for the future.[12]

Along with retiring earlier, the average worker is also living longer. The spectacular advances of medical science during this century have added years to the average life expectancy. Less than one hundred years ago one out of every twenty-five persons in the United States was over sixty-five. Presently one out of every ten is in this category. While the over-65 population in U.S. now numbers 20 million it is estimated this will increase to 29 million by the turn of the century. The potential for increased leisure is obvious.

Household conveniences

In the home automated appliances hand us an additional wealth of free-time potential. Where washing clothes once required a complete day of heating water, washing articles by hand, wringing and drying, the job is now done by machines. One can load the machine, push buttons, and proceed to other duties or to leisure. Washing machines and driers, dishwashers, ranges and ovens, refrigerators, steam irons, vacuum sweepers, and other conveniences reduce household chores. Kaplan estimates that automation gives modern homemakers the equivalent of ninety male servants.[13]

Improved transportation and communication
Another force in advancing leisure is the effect of rapid transportation and communication. The use of interstate highways and jet planes has greatly reduced travel time and thus has added to leisure-time potential. But, more important, these means of rapid transportation have greatly expanded the possibilities for the use of leisure through pleasure and vacation travel. The fantastic increase of travel abroad by Americans is a good example. With reference to communication, only marginal time is required now to conduct a visit or business by telephone or by other rapid means of transmitting messages.

Work-residence separation
Modern mass leisure is also enhanced by work-residence separation. Zoning laws and city planning have separated home and factory. When a worker leaves his factory after an eight-hour day, he is reasonably certain that he can put his job into the background until morning. Work makes no quantitative time demands when he is home. His work does not require his attention twenty-four hours a day as it did for his more rurally oriented great-grandfather.

The Advance of Leisure

All the above-mentioned factors — cybernation, productivity increases, shorter workweeks and years, more holidays, a longer life-span, postponement of work, earlier retirement, household conveniences, improved transportation and communication, and work-residence separation — add to the daily reservoir of free time. These are the forces of advancing leisure.

Perhaps the most impressive feature from a historical point of view concerns leisure's universality. Free time is not an entirely recent innovation. Leisure has existed since the beginning of history — existed, that is, in palaces, courtyards, country estates, and plantations. But the upper-class nobility and aristocracy were the sole possessors of the leisure commodity. Leisure for the masses was then and even now is a frightening prospect for the nobility. Bertrand Russell commented, "The idea of a four-hour workday shocks the well-to-do who are convinced that the poor don't have the capacity to use leisure, who only see leisure (for the masses) as a punishment for the unemployed."[14]

We have made a case thus far for the advance of free-time potential. It has been discussed, however, only from a quantitative point of view. By quoting the labor, production, and time statistics, the advance of leisure seems apparent. In quantitative terms we can be optimistic about leisure's potential both now and in the future.

5. The Retreating Horizon of Man's Response

In the simplest terms, the primary problem of leisure is how to avoid boredom. — *Russell Lynes*

For leisure to be qualitatively recreative man needs to be free — free from guilt about nonwork, free to be himself and to relax in his own way. True leisure is not a tense collapse from yesterday's toil merely to build strength for tomorrow's labors. Neither is leisure roving over the country in a recreational vehicle, fighting traffic jams with edgy tempers and bleary eyes. Modern social scientists are somewhat pessimistic about the chances for twentieth-century man to achieve quality leisure. One begins to understand Godby's phrase, "the retreating horizon."

Two major stumbling blocks plague the "Age of Leisure." They stem from two incorrect ways of looking at free time. The first regards it as time that must be crammed with activity or economically profitable exercise. The second considers free time as meaningless boredom. We shall analyze man's response to the age of leisure with these two factors in mind.

Pressures for leisure consumption

As cybernation increases productive capacity, industry needs to reach fresh markets with more and more new products. If factories can produce twice the goods in half the time, they need to create new wants or some will need to drastically curtail production. With work reductions and more free time on everyone's hands, it is natural that the business world looks to man's avocation for the sources of new markets. A leisure market for recreational equipment and services becomes a perfect area to create new products by capitalizing on man's fear of inactivity in his avocational time.

That the leisure market has enjoyed phenomenal growth is apparent. Yearly figures on the total sales of leisure products and services vary depending upon what is included as leisure. In the late sixties a major investment firm calculated leisure spending at $150 billion per year.[1]

A few figures will illustrate the trend in the development of leisure industries. More than 8,800,000 recreational boats of all kinds ply U.S. waters. The production of recreational camping vehicles increased more than 40 percent from 1961-1969. During the winter of 1969-70 American and Canadian firms produced half a million snowmobiles. Two million Americans own second homes and the number is climbing rapidly each year. It is estimated that over forty billion dollars is spent yearly in domestic pleasure and vacation travel.[2]

Charles Brightbill in his book, *The Challenge of Leisure*, accumulated some startling statistics concerning leisure spending. More money is spent in Florida on deep-sea fishing than the combined grosses of the state's citrus and cattle industries. Americans spend more money on dogs than the residents of Vermont earn as personal incomes. In one weekend skiers can pour more than $1 million dollars into a small New England town. In a single year Michigan licensed 61,000 people to hunt with bow and arrow.[3]

Without a doubt some of this phenomenal participation in leisure activities and spending represents fulfilling free-time enjoyment. But a thoughtful observer can note case after case of harried temperaments and unhappiness at America's countless entertainment spots. In the summertime many national parks look more like Times Square than back-to-nature areas. The rush to buy more, see more, do more, with more people reaches disease proportions every vacation time.

Why do many Americans persist in treating leisure time as madly busy consumption time? Twentieth-century man depends on the machine not only for material possessions, goods, items, and gadgets, but also for services and satisfaction. Money can buy everything according to Madison Avenue — health, friends, happiness, and a good leisure time. Leisure concerns are associated with spending money. We fail to understand that leisure requires the complete man, not simply man the spender, man the hurrier, or man the competitor.

Commercialization pervades all forms of leisure, from fad gadgets and devices to vacation developments and amusement parks. The modern American with a higher real income and newfound free time becomes a perfect target for leisure materialism. And because every leisure possession takes time to operate or enjoy, he finds himself lacking the one thing that money can't buy — time. Free time becomes busy time, harried time.

Eric Fromm pinpoints the problem of overconsumption. Man spends his time doing things in which he's not interested, with people in whom he's not interested, producing things in which he's not interested, and when he is not producing he is busy consuming. He is the eternal suckling with the open mouth. The man whose free time is that busy has no real leisure.[4]

Harried leisure time

Our modern competitive way of life becomes a second cause of busyness in leisure time. Modern industrialism has made work more concentrated and efficient. Although the average worker has more off-the-job hours, he cannot automatically switch gears from a world of time schedules and competition to a frame of mind conducive to leisure. Or if he can make the transition, his waking hours become shattered into two camps. His work and leisure become warring opposites.

Leisure in the modern industrial state is often seen as idleness or remoteness from reality, perhaps the Puritan ethic's ultimate victory.[5] All of man's time, even his so-called leisure time, becomes a slave to the ethic of production. Self-contained leisure time is decreed as wasted time.

Sociologists August Heckscher and Sebastian De Grazia studied patterns of executive leisure several years ago. They found that two thirds of their sample of executives considered off-duty time in church and charity activities as work. One third admitted that such activities increased their chances of promotion on the job.[6] Again, we find evidence that man mistrusts leisure that has no relation to his business or work life. However, for leisure to be important as recreation, man must realize its intrinsic worth.

Effects of moonlighting

Other facets of busyness in the new age of leisure are caused by moonlighting and auxiliary family wage earning. Sebastian De Grazia estimates that 10 percent of the jobholders who work over 35 hours a week on their first job have second jobs. Their second job adds an average of 12 more hours of work every week.[7] Therefore, if De Grazia's figures are correct, 10 percent of the American work force spends 47 to 60 hours on the job.

Moonlighting, ironically, increases as free-time potential increases. A classic example is the rubber capital of Akron, Ohio, where unions won a contract for a workweek of well under forty hours. Studies of the Akron area indicate that nearly 20 percent of the rubber workers hold second full-time jobs. Nearly half hold part-time occupations, usually in service jobs.

Two probable reasons for this phenomenon are expressed by Robert Lee. He surmises that workers find second jobs either to pay for increased leisure expenses or for the simple reason that most American workers are uncomfortable with too much free time.[8] French sociologist Jaffre Dumazedier's studies show that for 60 percent of the moonlighters, economic considerations have no role in the decision to take a second job.[9]

Auxiliary wage earning

Many families now have two jobholders. Health, Education, and Welfare statistics show that between 1950 and 1963 women's job participation in the age bracket of 20 to 64 rose 20.3 percent.[10] More recent statistics would probably show an even greater increase. As mentioned earlier, household conveniences have drastically reduced housework duties. Many women feel bored and trapped at home. Some make attempts to enjoy meaningful leisure but many seek a job that will fill their empty hours.

Most moonlighting jobs and more and more auxiliary wage earner's jobs are found in the area of service occupations. Although cybernation has replaced many workers engaged in the production of goods, many more workers are needed to repair the countless machines, gadgets, and vehicles that are considered essential to both our vocational and avocational pursuits. As more and more Americans travel, workers are needed to provide food and shelter for transitory guests, and to maintain transportation systems of all kinds for the hurried travelers.

Gilbert Burck reports that the service job index for the United States has risen 70 percent in the past twenty years — from 28 to 48 million.[11] Over one half of the work force is needed to provide for countless service needs. Although leisure time has enabled workers to purchase many goods and travel many miles, ironically the time it takes to service the goods and accommodate the travelers has threatened to snatch away the very leisure they thought they had possessed.

Commuting time loss

Job-residence separation, earlier mentioned as a boon to leisure potential, becomes a menace to free time in many urban areas. Busy highways not only pollute our external environment but also ruin the internal satisfaction of leisure living. The average modern commuter spends 1 1/2 hours every day fighting traffic to and from work. If he holds a second job he is often out on the road again after dinner or on weekends. With moonlighting statistics added, it is safe to assume that the average worker probably spends more than eight hours per week commuting to and from his job.[12] The worker who rises at dawn to catch his commuter train and returns to his home in the evening to give his children a good-night kiss has fair cause to wonder whether leisure has in fact made any gains since the beginning of the century.

Thus far we have discussed the threat that fast-paced living poses to the new leisure potential. We have mentioned and documented the trends toward harried avocational pursuits, moonlighting, auxiliary wage-earning, service needs, and commuting time loss. These factors all threaten meaningful recreative leisure. However, there is a second equally grave threat to true leisure living. This threat is boredom.

Boredom and the age of leisure

Earlier we mentioned various social groups who are being deleted from the work force because of cybernation's displacement of unskilled and semiskilled jobs. Cybernation's effects are first noticed in the fringe areas of the social structure — the elderly, the young, racial minorities, and the uneducated rural and urban poor. The free time that affluent citizens regard as at least potentially meaningful time becomes dead and meaningless time to those who have nothing to do. Enforced free time seldom becomes worthwhile leisure. To quote educator A. L. New, "One of the imperatives of the human spirit is: 'Act.' A situation that prevents human action is potentially explosive, it damages the very fibre of human being."[13]

The boredom of the unemployed can surface in various distressing forms — a discarded grandma withering away in a home for the aged, a teenage dropout who engages in crime for kicks, a frustrated ghetto dweller who has no means of transportation to reach the lucrative suburban jobs, the former Appalachian mine worker who waits on the porch of his tumbledown cabin for his welfare check. Enforced free time sometimes breeds meaningless violence, sometimes hollow nonliving. In either case, it is not leisure.

The unemployed by no means represent the only facet of society plagued by boredom. Emptiness and nonliving have regrettably pervaded all areas of modern society. We depend upon machines to think for us and act for us on our jobs. All too often we carry that dependence to our avocation. Charles Reich points out that our culture is made to be experienced passively:

A room in an expensive motel is a good example of impoverishment: a huge glass window with imposing draperies, wall-to-wall carpeting, air-conditioning, television, but nothing whatever to do — no books to read, no fire to be built in the fireplace, no place to cook, no records to be played. One can only sleep or let oneself be served, emerging with a flabby and diminished sense of self.[14]

The above quotation brings to mind Max Frisch's definition of technology as the knack of arranging the world so we don't have to experience it.[15] Several years ago Saunders and Parker asked a random sample of individuals to make lists of what they would ideally do in their leisure time. The participants listed swimming, tennis, boating, golf, camping, and gardening — activities which call for planning, organization, and active effort. Saunders and Parker then compiled time budgets which documented how their sample actually spent their leisure hours. This list included listening to the radio, watching television, reading magazines and newspapers, and going to movies or to friends' houses. The same persons who had hoped to fill their leisure time with active recreation in reality settled for more passive entertainment.[16]

We do not mean to imply that leisure time needs to be minutely planned to be effective and meaningful. Certainly, passive relaxation serves great benefits to the worker at the end of a busy workday. But much unfulfilled free time simply represents boredom and inertia, not real leisure happiness. To do nothing is beneficial if it represents the wishes of the person with leisure time. But if languor is merely a result of enforced leisure or if it is settled for as second best because of a lack of enthusiasm for life, then its leisure value is greatly suspect.

We have discussed future work-leisure patterns in terms of the advancing leisure potential both on and off the job. We have also examined the retreating horizon of meaningful resultant leisure. We have noted that leisure is stymied both by harried materialism and by the boredom and emptiness of unwanted, unfulfilled free time. Given these trends, what will characterize the age of leisure in the last quarter of this century and beyond? We shall offer some speculation based on the trends that have been already noted.

Central to any speculation about the future of work and leisure is the realization that we are moving into a post-industrial age. This age will probably differ as much from its predecessor as the industrial revolution differed from medieval agrarianism. The industrial age with its strong work ethic and its economic competition may not be realistic in an age where nearly all production is affected by cybernation.

Dr. Richard Bellman of Rand Corporation claims that within the next generation two percent of the population, with the help of machine thought and muscle, may be able to produce all the food and industrial products needed by the entire society. If such production is indeed feasible, it seems clear that the old values of the industrial society will be outdated. Such speculation may seem wild-eyed, but it is hardly impossible in an age where in one lifespan a person could have seen both the Wright brothers' first flight at Kitty Hawk and the first steps on the moon by the Apollo astronauts.

6. Work and Leisure in the Post-Industrial Age

Peace and prosperity are dangerous if a country doesn't know what to do with leisure. — *Sebastian De Grazia*

By projecting present trends it is possible to make predictions about the future. Applying this method to current work and leisure patterns gives us some idea of what the post-industrial age will be like. The production of goods and, to a lesser extent, service jobs will become automated. There will be a marked increase of leisure time but it will not affect all segments of the population alike. Two hypothetical family case studies will be used to describe how professionals and blue-collar workers will fare in the post-industrial society.

Professionals in the age of leisure

Mr. Smith is a successful lawyer. His wife works part time as a journalist and is active in political and civic interests. The Smiths who have professional service jobs are just as busy as ever, for the post-industrial age is indeed a service age. Paradoxically, in the future it seems that the upper professional classes will be much busier than the blue-collar workers. Already the age-old rule that leisure accompanies wealth has been reversed.

With the increasing specialization and complexity of modern urban society, almost everyone needs legal services and Mr. Smith is increasingly busy. Mrs. Smith finds plenty of work writing articles for the numerous magazines and newspapers that have sprung up to absorb modern leisure time and spending. When the Smiths finally get away from their duties they feel guilty simply sitting at home. Often they spend their evenings partying with business contacts or working in civic clubs.

Blue-collar workers in the age of leisure

Mr. Jones, a blue-collar worker, is employed on the assembly line of a furniture factory near his home. He is a member of a union which has recently won a four-week paid vacation every year. And there's talk at the factory that the management may experiment with a three-day weekend or a six-hour day. Some of Mr. Jones' fellow workers have even heard that employees with over twenty years' seniority may be required to take a summer's leave every third year. Automation has already dried up many of the jobs on the production line and Mr. Jones is becoming uneasy about the stability of his own job.

Mrs. Jones finds that her new household appliances

have shortened her workday. Since several of the children have left home she has less and less family chores. Now and then an uneasy boredom sets in. Since she doesn't like to read, she watches daytime serials on television. When her husband comes home her boredom and irritation often surface.

Unfortunately, Mr. Jones gets little real satisfaction from his job. Like his father and grandfather he makes furniture, but unlike his craftsman ancestors he never sees the finished product. He simply pushes a button on a machine which planes table legs as they travel through the assembly line. When he gets home in the evening to take advantage of the extra leisure hours his union contract has won for him, he just can't seem to find anything to do. So he watches television.

Admittedly, we have stereotyped the Smiths and the Joneses. Yet the trends they represent are quite predictable. It is obvious that the realities of the post-industrial age affect these families in differing ways.

To continue the comparison, Charles Reich in *The Greening of America* has written a portrait of our Mr. Smith's harried professional life:

> A young boy asks his father, "What do you do, Daddy?" Here is how the father might answer: "I struggle with crowds, traffic jams, and parking problems for about an hour. I talk a great deal on the telephone to people I hardly know. I dictate to a secretary and then proofread what she types. I have all sorts of meetings with people I don't know very well or like very much. I eat lunch in a big hurry and can't taste or remember what I've

eaten. I hurry, hurry, hurry. I spend my time in very functional furniture, and I never look at the weather or sky or people passing by. I talk but I don't sing or dance or touch people. I spend the last hour, all alone, struggling with crowds, traffic, parking." Now this same father might also answer: "I am a lawyer. I help people and businesses solve their problems. I help everybody to know the rules that we all have to live by, and to get along according to these rules." Both answers are "true." Why is the first truth less recognized than the second?[1]

Arthur Schlesinger, Jr., has summarized the situation of the Joneses just as succinctly:

Those [members of the lower-middle and working classes] who are likely to have the most free time in a high-technology society are also those who, through no fault of their own, are often least trained by education and environment to use free time wisely and creatively — to convert free time into genuine leisure. The dilemma, in short, is that those whose minds and lives are least prepared for the ordeal of leisure are the ones who are going to have the most of it. [2]

Schlesinger goes on to cite a Gallup Poll which finds that 58 percent of the American population have never finished reading a book, excepting a textbook or the Bible. Already our society spends a phenomenal amount of time watching television. This is not to say that television is totally unfulfilling leisure, but undoubtedly it aims its programming to the average or popular taste. And the commercialization which accompanies and complements the programs provides the mass audience with what Schlesinger calls a "standardized fantasy life." [3] In short, television seems to epitomize the kind of leisure culture which, as we mentioned above, is meant to be experienced passively with little active initiative or spontaneity.

Ernest Haveman further describes Mr. Jones' dilemma as the post-industrial society begins to crumble the foundations of industrial security. "What happens to a worker who suddenly finds himself with so much free time in one chunk? Does he pack up his wife and children and take them on a trip? (Thirteen weeks of travel would cost him a fortune.) Does he putter around the house all that time? Can he fill his idle time effectively?" [4]

The retreating leisure horizon

Although the dilemmas of the Smith and Jones families are somewhat different, perhaps there are common roots for their problems. It seems that one problem central to both families is that their capacity for leisure was educated out of them at an early age by an industrial ethnic based on work, competition, and economic reward. As Haveman points out, from kindergarten on, education is given a highly utilitarian flavor. Hard work and study are necessary not for any leisure benefits but rather to get ahead in the world. One studies English in order to write a business letter, not for the purpose of reading great literature. Income-tax forms necessitate studying math; little attention is paid to its intrinsic beauty. [5] The question before us then is whether or not industrial ethics, in education or otherwise, can fulfill the needs of man in a post-industrial age.

Let us take Mr. Jones' case even further. Suppose his worst fears are realized and a computer is installed which can determine exactly when a table leg must be planed and can activate the planer automatically. Mr. Jones would then be out of a job. The industrial ethics of survival-of-the-fittest economic competition and profit motivation would necessitate the factory's firing Mr. Jones. In the face of phenomenal cybernetic advances and a post-industrial society, can the old industrial ethic still be just?

Bertrand Russell addresses himself to this very question in his characteristically gruff manner.

> Suppose a certain number of people make pins. They can fulfill the world's need for pins working an eight-hour day. Someone invents a machine which doubles the speed of pin-making. But the world does not need twice as many pins; pins are already so cheap that no more will be bought at a lower price. In a sensible world the pin-makers would work four hours instead of eight and everything would be as before. But not in our leisure-frightened world. The men still work eight hours, there are twice as many pins, some employers go bankrupt, half of the pin-makers are out of work. In the end there is just as much leisure but half are totally idle while the other half are overworked . . . When these devices fail, we have a war and keep one-half busy making explosives and the other half busy exploding them. . . . In this way unavoidable leisure causes misery all around because men are afraid to plan for sensible leisure. Can anything more insane be imagined?[6]

A second response that industrial economic ethics offers to the post-industrial cybernation and leisure revolution is the creation of false wants and planned obsolescence. Let us relate this specifically to Mr. and Mrs. Smith. Both of them spend the bulk of their recreational efforts in activities which did not even exist years ago. They rush from sports car rallies to German shepherd dog shows. They are examples of what Robert MacIver calls the go-getters and power-seekers.[7] They seek success rather than life itself. They join cultural societies not for the joy of experiencing great art but in order to be seen with the right people at the right places. They buy a new $9,000 car, not because their old one is worn out, but to maintain their social position. They buy a travel bus, not because they enjoy the leisure of camping, but so they can join the same travel club to which Mr. Smith's business associates belong. Caught in the sequence of excitement, hollow release, and boredom, the Smiths represent what MacIver terms "a sequence of brief delusions of escape, not real leisure."[8]

The effect of this constant rapid cultural change is numbing. Again quoting Reich, "A hasty French meal, a new building going up to replace one just twenty years old, coast-to-coast travel in a few hours, new models of cars and appliances before the character of the old is known, all of these diminish meaning, sensitivity, and awareness."[9]

In both the Smiths' and Joneses' cases we see the advancing leisure potential of a post-industrial age vainly chasing a retreating horizon. As long as we face the post-industrial society with the industrial morality of a narrow work ethic, competition, materialism, and the virtue of busyness, the horizon will continue to retreat.

Possibilities for a new leisure ethic

Yet, there may be another way, a way that will treat the coming leisure revolution not with fear and agitated busyness, nor with languor and meaningless boredom, but with acceptance and happiness. Both Mr. Smith and Mr. Jones could face their post-industrial society with a new readiness to treat leisure as a congenial companion.

In planning for the new leisure society, that readiness would accept the virtue of intrinsic excellence rather than externally imposed status. It would lead to cooperation between those in the dwindling production jobs and the rapidly increasing service occupations so that every person would be able to participate in both creative work and meaningful leisure. It would subvert the old industrial morality's way of measuring a man's worth by the amount of goods and services he could produce. Men would no longer be judged either by their ability to put nose to grindstone or by leisure possessions. Given even a small measure of post-industrial leisure-receptive mentality, both the Smiths and the Joneses could make large strides toward filling their lives with creative activity both in their vocation and their avocation. Mr. Smith could treat his law vocation more as a real service to society than a status occupation. He could train legal aides to help him with his many duties, thereby shortening his own work load and helping other unemployed citizens find meaningful opportunities. He could refuse to let himself and his wife be turned into status objects. They could rid themselves of some of the external gadgets which bring no real leisure — only headaches and expense. They could learn how to appreciate art, activities, and civic affairs for their own worth rather than their external value in society.

Mr. Jones, with his newfound spare time, could relearn the art of creating the fine furniture of his ancestors. Released from the need to gain economic stability by producing faster, cheaper, and more mechanistically, Mr. Jones could capture the joy of creative labor. Because his labor would be more meaningful, his life would cease to be the uneasy reconciliation of two warring opposites and both his vocation and avocational joy of living would prosper. Mrs. Jones could realize that education is more than simply a ticket to a job and would thus be free to return to an educational environment which might train her for some new vocational skills and leisure-time activities.

But to affect these changes, both couples will need to realize that the pursuit of pleasure is in itself no vice. Both will need to learn the joys of creative work and meaningful leisure. Both will need to pay special attention to a leisure ethic more befitting a post-industrial age.

III. The Anatomy of Work — The Work Ethic

7. *Work and Its Meaning*

If it were desired to reduce a man to nothing, it would be necessary only to give his work a character of uselessness. — *Fyodor Dostoevski*

According to Wayne E. Oates of Southern Baptist Theological Seminary many people are hooked on work. They suffer from "workaholism — the uncontrollable need to work incessantly." In his book, *Confessions of a Workaholic,* Professor Oates described his own addiction to work. Having been hooked for nearly thirty years, he managed to kick the habit in 1966. [1]

A workaholic is one who "drops out of human community and eats, drinks, and sleeps his job." [2] His time, indeed his whole life, is highly work-oriented and regulated. Demanding peak performance of himself and of others, he is a compulsive activist. His fantasies of omnipotence lead him to imagine that no one but he can do what needs doing.

It is not difficult to imagine how a work-obsessed person feels about leisure. Leisure is a gross waste of time. Any recreational use of time is highly begrudged. If he wasn't sure that some rest and diversion were necessary for health reasons and for the continuance of peak work performance, he would gladly skip recreation altogether. He feels guilty about using time for leisure and assuages that guilt the only way he knows how — through more work.

Psychiatrist Francis L. Clark speaks of this phenomenon as follows:

> There is the stockbroker who takes his first vacation in five years, lasts two days at the beach, and becomes so anxious that he returns home.
> The lawyer who takes up woodworking as a hobby, and then works at it compulsively, his electric saw still humming in the dawn hours.
> The medical student who feels guilty about "wasting" an afternoon watching a football game.
> The housewife who insists upon bringing the children on every outing with her husband so she can keep busy cooking and caring for them.
> This type of person is a work freak. Work is his whole life and he can't seem to enjoy anything else. He can no more give up work than an alcoholic can give up booze. [3]

A contrasting situation, "the endless weekend," was described in a special issue of *LIFE* concerning Americans at play. Resulting from a combination of shorter workweek, greater affluence among workers, and the deadening meaninglessness of many jobs, the status of the weekend has become increasingly important. *LIFE* said:

Work and Its Meaning

> Nowadays you can't define the weekend in terms of the gap between Friday night and Monday morning. The weekend is a state of mind, betrayed by a vacant stare that lasts till Tuesday and an anticipatory twitching that begins on Thursday. We talk fishing at the factory, surfing at the store, skiing in the office, and when we make new acquaintances we identify ourselves less by what we do for a living than by what we do to loaf. . . . Wherever we are, inside our heads we're *out there*. [4]

These people, too, are hooked. Leisure, the welcome escape, is epitomized in the endless weekend.

The meanings of work

Such illustrations suggest that a clue to one's views about leisure can be found through understanding his experiences and feelings about work. This is particularly true since work has been the dominant theme in our culture. According to this thesis, leisure derives its meaning in relation to work. Therefore, to understand contemporary views of leisure, it is necessary to investigate the anatomy of work. This will be attempted through a further analysis of the meaning of work in our society, the historical patterns of work, and the development of the work ethic.

Because of our common experience, work is a familiar concept. In everyday terminology, work, labor, and toil, mean much the same thing. Labor has the sense of strenuous physical exertion. At least in the past, this described quite adequately what the word meant. Toil, which suggests the drudgery and travail of hard work, has an almost painful ring to it. On the other hand, work is a broad and comprehensive term with many meanings. The Scriptures speak of "the work of our hands," "the work of God," "good works," and "their works do follow them." In fact the usages of the term are so varied that it would require a long listing to cover all of its meanings. This difficulty of precise definition is rooted in the fact that work, like leisure, is also a socially defined term. Its meanings vary according to the cultural setting in which it is embedded,

Providing life's necessities

Why does man work? At the most elemental level he works to provide the necessities of life. Since nature yields up her provisions for food, clothing, and shelter with reluctance, much labor is required. While we are less aware in our sophisticated society of the work demands needed to provide the necessities of life, the requirement is still there. In the areas of the world where hunger and poverty are ever-present, this day-to-day struggle for sustenance is a grim reality of life for millions of people.

Maintaining a standard of living

In addition to basic subsistence, man also works to achieve and maintain a certain standard of living. For modern man this standard makes work as important as ever. Sebastian De Grazia developed in his classic volume, *Of Time, Work, and Leisure*, the thesis that man today is basically a consumer. We work not only to obtain the things we need but also the things we want. These things cost money, money costs work, and work costs time. [5] Our American economy involves most of us in an upwardly mobile standard of living. It is work which provides the gadgets and services of the good life.

Satisfying psychological needs

Another reason for work is its psychological benefits. Man responds to such factors as pride in performing a task well done, establishing a sense of personal worth, or a satisfaction in creating or producing something out of nature into something of his own making. Mortimer Adler speaks of the operative and cooperative arts of man. In the one case human effort is applied on nature to bring about some desired effect which nature itself cannot achieve, such as the cobbler operating upon rawhide to produce a pair of shoes. Cooperative arts, on the other hand, put man in cooperation with nature to assist and facilitate its customary procedures. The medical doctor who assists the natural physiological processes to restore health is an example of this. In both cases the fulfillment of these arts can be of great human satisfaction.[6]

Work establishes an identification and a status since a man's sense of worth is frequently tied directly to the job he holds. In many cases there is a social satisfaction which comes from associating with others on the job. Retired employees testify that they sorely miss this sense of comradeship after they leave their jobs and subsequently find themselves alone.

The human satisfaction inherent in work is reflected in the following quotations. The first is from a psychiatrist at Rockland State Mental Hospital, Orangeburg, New York: "Most people in our culture work — if they're fortunate — not just to make money, but because they derive satisfaction from what they are doing. We have needs that our work helps us fulfill. Power, visibility, they are almost too numerous to mention."[7] From another orientation Karl Marx observed:

> Labor is the very touchstone for man's self-realization, the medium of creating the world of his desire; and it is the labor which should make him happy. Indeed, the essence of man is in his striving to achieve his desires. He labors to transform his world, to put his own mark on it, to make it his, and to make himself at home in it.[8]

Promising future benefits

Man works also because of a kind of deferred benefit, a future-time orientation. Work promises the possibilities of doing other things, the things which we like and are free to choose. C. Wright Mills tells about the men "who sell little pieces of their lives in order to buy them back each night with the coin of fun."[9] The anticipations of holidays, vacations, and leisure-time activities are strong incentives. The TGIF (Thank God It's Friday) philosophy is more than a passing slogan for most workers. Work is the medium by which we obtain certain promised rewards, both material and nonmaterial.

Contrary to the prevailing work ethic, work may be oriented to play as much as, if not more than, it is for the sake of earning a livelihood. It may be the nonwork activities which lend to work such meanings as it has. Robert S. Cohen notes that Karl Marx reminded us of this inverted work morality found in modern Western civilization in these words:

> Labor has been turned into a grinding chore, instead of the medium of human fulfillment. Work has been made an ignoble means to something alien to and outside it, to wit: leisure. It is leisure, we think, which is the real end of life; work is just a degrading necessity. [10]

Supplying moral satisfactions

One more, and quite a contrasting motivation, is the moral satisfaction which may be attached to one's work. To the person who believes that he has been called to his work by God or by the church, the religious motivation is strong. If a particular work has been invested with sacred significance, it will be considered as good and pursued with pride, diligence, and **loyalty. Rewards for faithful labor** are promised both in this world and the next. In its extreme form, work may amount to a kind of divinely ordained system of measuring and rewarding human worth.

These considerations about the meaning of work serve as foundation for understanding the work ethic. It is certain that the motivations which induce the average person to work are quite complex. Human action, certainly work, is seldom prompted by a single motive. In most instances several of these reasons may underlie a man's efforts. Likely he is not fully aware of all that is driving him to his daily toil.

An important work

Since this discussion about work has presupposed the remunerative eight-to-five type of job, it is important to recognize another segment of work — the responsibility of the homemaker. Marriage is an institution ordained by God and millions of women devote full time to the work of homemaker. Others carry a remunerative job in addition to their homemaking duties. In many cases homemaking is a shared activity by husband and wife.

The task of parent and homemaker is tied directly to God's mandate for work as given in the Genesis creation account. The fact that a homemaker's work is usually not defined in terms of a forty-hour week or a monthly salary check does not detract, but rather enhances its importance.

The homemaker fulfills in a unique way the varied purposes set forth for work in this chapter. Likewise, the discussions to follow on the work ethic, the leisure ethic, and the need to prepare oneself for the leisure age apply with just as much importance to the homemaker as to the jobholder. In fact, homemaking has opportunities not equaled by any other kind of work for integrating work and leisure into a meaningful life for parents and children.

8. God's People and Work

Leisure and I have parted company. I am resolved to be busy till I die. — *John Wesley*

Work in the Old Testament

Work is rooted in God's creation as a divinely instituted element of human existence. A pattern of work was set by God in the six days of creative activity. God worked to produce the world, "and he rested on the seventh day from all his work which he had made."[1] The interpretation that work in this usage does not refer to "toil" but rather to His "fashioning" of the world does not violate the meaning of work in its best sense, that of creative activity.

Immediately after creating man in His own image God gave to man a work assignment. "Be fruitful and multiply, and fill the earth and subdue it; and have dominion over the fish of the sea and over the birds of the air and over every living thing that moves upon the earth."[2] Work is in accordance with an eternal divine plan. Man is to subdue the earth and draw out its potentialities for his own good. Every worker, whether he deals with natural or human resources, shares in fulfilling God's work command. In effect the command is to cooperate with God in the continuance of His work in creation. Human work is the counterpart of divine work.

While the Fall of man brought the curse of toil and hardship and perverted man's attitude toward his labors, the divine blessing upon work was not degraded. There were to be thorns and thistles and man was to earn his bread by the sweat of his face. "Six days shalt thou labour, and do all thy work."[3] "Man goeth forth unto his work and to his labour until the evening."[4]

Thus, in the Old Testament work was in the purpose of God for man. Not only should man work to supply the necessities of life, but work was an essential expression of his nature as man, made in the image of God the Creator. Furthermore, it is God who gives the strength for labor, provides the goods upon which man can work, and supplies the rewards. "And be strong, all ye people of the land, saith the Lord, and work: for I am with you, saith the Lord of hosts."[5]

Work in the early Christian church

While the New Testament says little about work, it does elaborate on some of its social dimensions. The worker was to receive an adequate remuneration for his efforts.[6] The Apostle Paul scorns the loafer, "that if any would not work, neither should he eat."[7] In his own life he set the example of economic self-sufficiency. "Neither did we eat any man's bread for nought; but wrought with labour and travail night and day, that we might not be chargeable to any of you."[8] He urged his followers to work with their own hands.[9] Not only does work help one to provide for his own, but also it makes possible the means to support others who are in need.[10] Both the Old and New Testaments seem to underline the morality of a good day's work.

Otto A. Piper[11] states that the church in the early centuries continued to view work as a necessity of life. By the sixth century St. Benedict prescribed work as a spiritual discipline. Cloister bells sounded calling the brothers to pray and likewise summoning them to work with their hands. The Benedictine motto, "To labor is to pray" emphasized the divine sanction which had been given to work.

Sacred and secular work

In the Middle Ages Thomas Aquinas presented work as the law of nature. Work was part of the divine scheme of things. Work was a right; no man could live without working; therefore, the social order was to provide opportunities of work for all. Furthermore, work enabled a person to give alms and thus to acquire merit.

Of greater historic influence on the ethic of work, Aquinas differentiated men into classes and occupations and rated work in terms of the value of goods produced. The special calling of the monks and the spiritual activities of monastic life were regarded as superior to all secular forms of work. There came to be a strong sacred-secular work dichotomy. In the Thomistic view a man's life was divided into two spheres, devoted either to spiritual ends or to economic pursuits.

All work is sacred

The Reformation brought a change of outlook which has influenced the meaning of work ever since. The concept of vocation (God's calling to His service) was broadened to include the "callings of the common life" as contrasted with the earlier and more narrow special calling of the monk. As Max Weber once wrote, "The whole world became a monastery and every man a monk."[12] As protesters against the Catholic Church's claim to be the only authentic interpreter of God's laws, Martin Luther and John Calvin became the crucial figures in this new religious-social-political economy.

It seems clear, however, that Luther and Calvin did not set out as such to be social revolutionaries, nor political-economic reformers. Their primary concern was with man's redemption and his ultimate loyalty and destiny. They did not consciously formulate a Protestant ethic of work. Rather, the patterns of action which developed were derived from their theological interpretations. Albert Rasmussen speaks of the sources of their motivations and deep convictions as follows:

> These men were double respondents, as are all Christian reinterpreters of the Christian faith and its claims upon men. They were respondents to the historic situation in

which they lived, which they regarded as corrupt and in discontinuity with the Biblical faith. And they measured this corruption and discontinuity by their even more focal response to the abiding source and center of their faith, the disclosing event of Christ as cradled in the Biblical Scriptures.[13]

In the practical outworking of their beliefs, these Reformers applied the concept of vocation (God's calling) to the ordinary jobs and employments of life. As noted, they rejected the medieval view that monastic pursuits were an exclusive expression of divine calling and thus in a separate category from secular work. In effect they brought a union between man's vocation and his work. Roland Bainton says, "Luther declared that the Gospel could be exemplified only in the midst of secular callings, only Luther refused to call them secular. As he had extended the priesthood of all believers, so likewise he extended the concept of divine calling, vocation, to all worthy occupations."[14]

Thomas F. Green claims a difference, at least in degree, between the view of Luther and Calvin on work. According to Luther, one expressed his vocation (religious calling) *in* his work (station or office). Calvin believed that one's vocation was expressed *through* his work.[15] While this difference in prepositional phrases may not have great significance, it does suggest a contrast of meaning in their views about work. Calvin's view of vocation was more dynamic than Luther's view.

Luther believed that a man's vocation was to be carried out within the orders of the common life where God had placed him. God had no other hands and feet. Whether a man was a peasant, magistrate, teacher, or prince the vocation (calling) was to be exercised in that particular station of life. Luther was quick to defend those labors which for one reason or another were disparaged. The lowlier the task, the better; in that pre-industrial age the premium was on physical labor. The milkmaid and the farmhand were doing a work just as pleasing to God as the psalm-singing of the most austere monastic order.

With John Calvin the union between vocation and work became even stronger. The Christian not only lives out his calling *in* his work but also *through* his work. In effect, a man's vocation is his work. His job is the expression of his calling. For all practical purposes, vocation and work were now fully equated. "From here it is a small step, indeed, to the view that the meaning of a man's life is his job. It is through his job that a man discovers his contentment and defines who he is."[16] Thus the basic tenets of the Protestant work ethic were formulated.

The Protestant work ethic

Max Weber in the early 1900s developed his classic theory linking Protestantism and capitalism together. He observed that it was in the Protestant countries that capitalism made its swiftest headway and that from among Calvinists and Puritans had come the preponderance of new entrepreneurs. Capitalism had become the social counterpart of Calvinist theology.[17] Rasmussen describes the Calvinist influence this way:

Calvinism contributed a doctrine of Christian calling or vocation that not only removed the Christian stigma and lack of full legitimacy of the medieval church toward material production but made it into a sacred calling — a ministry — to the glory of God and of Christ. It provided both a moral and sacred legitimacy, but even beyond that, a sense of holy and dedicated purpose.[18]

To the Calvinist the calling was a serious and exacting enterprise to be chosen by himself and to be pursued with a sense of religious responsibility. Work was not only an economic means, but a spiritual end. Each man was under obligation to work hard for his own election's sake. To be on earth was to be responsible to work.

One can note in the Calvinistic work ethic a set of strong, but somewhat conflicting motivations. On the one hand was an intense devotion to hard work and the production of goods; on the other hand, a dedication to frugal, prudent living. Developing as a middle-class movement its value system stressed piety, industry, and thrift.

It is of interest to note in passing that Max Weber commented on the combination of the religious way of life and the intensive development of business acumen which characterized the Quakers and the Mennonites, both of whom were known for their otherworldliness and wealth. For instance in East Prussia, Frederick William I tolerated the Mennonites as indispensable to industry in spite of their absolute refusal to accept military service.[19] Donald Royer who writes on the Church of the Brethren economic ethic makes the observation that "the Brethren and Mennonites in

America appeared to pursue with even greater intensity and devotion the economic activities of life than did the Calvinists, probably as a result of their social and political isolationism."[20]

The Puritan work ethic

Another chapter in the development of the Protestant work ethic took place on the shores of Colonial New England. Operating under Calvinist convictions, the Puritans set up a theocracy in this bleak new world. They believed the rule of God was to be evident in all affairs of life including the economic processes. In Puritan society work was legitimized as a means of glorifying God and was held up as a defense against idleness and waste of time. Diligence, thrift, and sobriety were cardinal virtues. Man's accountability was rooted in his responsibilities for time, possessions, and stewardship. He would be judged according to the faithfulness by which he employed these gifts for mankind and for God.

In Puritan literature and folklore one finds many admonitions exalting work, as well as warnings against idleness. Among the tales is that of a Puritan woman who was waiting in a darkened room for the funeral services to her deceased husband to begin. Not wishing to waste a minute in idleness she whispered to her daughter, "Pass me my knitting. I might knit a few bouts while the folks are gathering."[21] Aside from the therapy values of work in situations of grief, the point of this incident probably speaks more to the prevailing Puritan ethic of work.

An Old Sturbridge Village (Massachusetts) reprint of

God's People and Work

a Boston *Evening News* item, dated October 9, 1769, sets forth a good example for all readers.

> FEMALE INDUSTRY, Woodstock, Conn., Aug. 18th. The following remarkable instance of industry lately happened here, and we hope will stimulate others to imitate actions so truly laudable. The wife of Mr. Stephen Rogers milk'd 8 cows in the morning — made her cheeses — turned and took care of fourscore cheeses — made a number of beds — swept her house, consisting of three rooms — spun six skains of worsted yarn — baked a batch of bread — churned a quantity of butter — and milked 7 cows in the Evening.[22]

Rasmussen summarizes the Puritan attitude about work:

> The three great motifs of Reformed Protestantism were central themes in their self-understanding. These were "calling," "holy worldliness," and "God's active rule." They were on a chartered mission to which they had been called by God himself. This mission for their lives was "worldly," to be fulfilled in serving him in "a hideous and desolate wilderness" as he had opened the door of history for them.[23]

Coupled with the work ethic of the Puritans was the fact that life in the wilderness placed upon the settlers exacting demands simply to exist. The need to survive put a high premium on labor for all. It took hard work to clear the forest, raise food, build shelter, and provide protection. As long as the frontier existed in American history, strenuous physical labor was a stark necessity for most people. Thus, a rugged and simple gospel of work was particularly suited to a wilderness-taming, westerly moving generation of pioneers. "Work, for the Night Is Coming" has been an American marching song for over a century.

This dedication to hard work and dependence upon nature for livelihood and prosperity can be illustrated in the lives of our own rural forefathers. A fall's harvest was contingent upon a spring and summer's nourishing rain and sun. A flood, tornado, drought, or insect plague could easily ravage crops and ruin a farmer's year financially. Since the godly farmer believed that nature and the seasons were ruled by divine power, it was natural for him to petition in prayer for good growing weather.

After harvest, as the hard-working family sat around bountiful tables, the farmer gave thanks to God for well-filled barns. Indirectly he was also thanking God for the resultant well-filled wallet. One can easily understand how hard work and prosperity became the signs of God's favor and the reward for a life of Christian obedience and austerity.

Contributions of the work ethic

The Protestant work ethic emphasized a number of significant principles and implications. Man has been placed on earth to glorify God, to do the works of Him that sent him while it is yet day. Waste of time is thus a sin; slothfulness and idleness are a reflection on God's grace. St. Paul's injunction that all should work includes the wealthy as well. Wealth, in itself, is not ethically wrong as long as it is the result of conscientious effort and does not lead to idleness and sinful enjoyment.

It remained for John Wesley to speak forthrightly concerning a lifestyle characterized by hard work and thriftiness. "We ought not to prevent people from being diligent and frugal; we must exhort all Christians to gain all they can, and to save all they can; that is, in effect, to grow rich."[24] Then follows the advice that those who have gained all they can and saved all they can should give all they can. In this way they were able to grow in grace and store up treasures in heaven.

Along with its principles there are also some durable strains of action bound up in the Protestant work ethic. The identification of one's Christian calling with one's work has been a powerful incentive for good craftsmanship. Even the most menial tasks should and can be done well. In Western culture we have confidence in the work which another does for us, whether he be auto mechanic, postman, or dentist. The work ethic has provided many people with meaning, identification, and fulfillment in their jobs or professions. Work is dignified and the worker is given a favorable status in our culture. The men who go to work in the morning and come home at night are still the pillars of society.[25]

In 1939 a newspaper columnist from the Midwest made a striking statement about work in a syndicated article. To what extent does his statement reflect the traditional Protestant view of work? To what degree does he articulate basic attitudes we hold about work?

> Work is divine. God is revealed as the great worker and it is through work that men become like God. It is

through work that man finds his life and his life is measured by his work. Business is a means by which men exchange usefulness. In the exchange of commodities and services both parties are benefited, both parties profit. The more a man is given the more he receives. To run away from work is to run away from life. To repudiate work is to commit suicide.[26]

9. A Critical Look at the Traditional Work Ethic

Lost, yesterday, somewhere between sunrise and sunset, two golden hours, each set with sixty diamond minutes. No reward is offered, for they are gone forever. — *Horace Mann*

Secularization of the Protestant work ethic

Historically a number of elements converged to modify the influence of the historic Protestant work ethic and to shape a more secularized view of work. Benjamin Franklin found the Puritan virtues of work and thrift valuable but separated them from the faith which had contained them. Hard work and frugality were important in their own right and had their own worldly rewards. Franklin's work-thrift doctrine was most effectively expressed in his *Advice to Young Tradesmen* and *Necessary Hints to Those That Would Be Rich*. Here is a sample of his economic truisms:

> Time is money.
> Waste not, want not.
> Diligence overcomes difficulties, sloth makes them.
> Get what you can and what you get, hold; 'tis a stone that will turn all your lead into gold.
> I never went ahunting or afishing. It was profitable at least to appear frugal before my clients.
> In order to secure my character and credit as a tradesman, I took care not only to be in reality industrious and frugal, but to avoid the appearance of the contrary. I dressed plain and was seen at no places of idle diversion. [1]

The intellectuals of Franklin's day and later were influenced by the Enlightenment of France and the other European countries. Its deistic rationalism put man at the center of the stage. Man was thought to be self-sufficient and through moral striving, intellectual exercise, and hard work, the world was his. Rudyard Kipling spoke for man in Western culture when he wrote:

> If you can fill the unforgiving minute
> With sixty seconds' worth of distance run —
> Yours is the Earth and everything that's in it
> And — which is more — you'll be a Man, my son! [2]

Free enterprise and the notion of *laissez faire* (the absence of governmental regulation and interference) became dominant influences in economic theory. Man was placed on a good and fruitful world; he had merely to roll up his sleeves and make the most of it. [3]

A contemporary acknowledgment of this same kind of work conscience was stated in recent autobiographical writing by Arnold J. Toynbee, the noted historian.

A Criticzl Look at the Tradidional Work Ethic

> In my attitude about work I am American-minded. To be always working and still at full stretch has been laid upon me by my conscience as a duty. This enslavement to work for work's sake is, I suppose, irrational; but thinking so would not liberate me. If I slacked or even just slackened, I would be conscience-stricken and therefore uneasy and unhappy, so this spur seems likely to continue to drive me on so long as I have any working power left in me. [4]

As the predominately agrarian society moved toward an industrialized, urban society the work ethic further emerged into a "gospel of wealth." This term, popularized by Andrew Carnegie in the title of his autobiography, stressed wealth as a motivation for diligent application to work. Through wealth, man could greatly extend his influence for good. In Russell Conwell's lecture, "Acres of Diamonds," which was delivered over 6,000 times, men were urged to get rich as the test of their usefulness in the world. The social evolutionary theories of Herbert Spencer gave further support to the view that man succeeds by his own efforts. Through a free and unhampered pursuit of wealth the strong succeed and the weak and slothful fall by the way.

In summarizing the creed which underlies the gospel of wealth ethic Albert T. Rasmussen notes the following points which he garnered from *The American Business Creed* by Francis X. Sutton and three colleagues (Harvard University Press, 1956):

1. Central emphasis on the individual
2. Self-reliance
3. Productivity: volume of material production as the

chief measure of well being
4. Activism as the most honored way of life
5. Progress as chief goal and hope
6. Optimism as the only valid personal and historical attitude
7. Competition as the key regulator of the economic system
8. Consumer sovereignty as ruler of production
9. Self-interest or the profit motive as the decisive incentive in human effort [5]

If these principles do, indeed, represent the modern work ethic, we can agree with Rasmussen that "the demise and reversal of the Reformed view was virtually complete; the shambles that was left was christened with the euphemistic and wholly contradictory title, "The Protestant Ethic."[6] Perhaps a better designation for the phenomena it describes would be the gospel of hard work. "Disciplined work had become the secular substitute for religious devotion."[7]

The work ethic under question

Increasingly, the Protestant work ethic as traditionally interpreted is being challenged by Christian thinkers today. Gordon J. Dahl writing in *The Christian Century* says:

> . . . it is high time we pointed out that the so-called "Protestant ethic" was bad religion in the first place, and that in its modern secular form as the "work ethic" it is a superstition that sanctifies violence and exploitation. Surely we realize that high profits or high wages are the result of governmental subsidies or aggressive unions rather than of any personal achievement or divine tinkering. Surely we realize that the miseries of today's poor and

oppressed outrage the moral order. Yet, piously perverse, we allow the superstition to influence our private attitudes and our public policy. [8]

John Drescher in a *Gospel Herald* editorial expressed a similar judgment:

> Perhaps no other one thing has so deeply discredited the Christian church as her unquestioning submission to the economic theory of society. In fact, the church is probably as guilty as any organization of society for putting its stamp of approval on the economic theory rampant today. Because the church has stressed the idea that if one works hard and is frugal God will, because of this, give both contentment and prosperity, the church has helped encourage an enlightened self-interest in its vulgarest forms. [9]

Both writers are suggesting that despite new dilemmas arising in economic life we are still tied to an old work theory which reflects the mixture of both Protestant ethic and secularized gospel of hard work. It is time for a reexamination of attitudes and actions, particularly in light of a basic Christian view. Drescher calls for a Christian doctrine of work "which speaks as the Scripture does to the employer, to the employee, to the purpose of work, and to the kinds of work a Christian is called to do and what he can and cannot produce." [10]

While the Protestant ethic of work still influences our thinking there is little question but that it is losing its grip. Contemporary devotion to the sanctity of work in America is more a lip service than a reality. The dignity of hard work for its own sake is under question. The old work ethic as a way of life is in trouble. In an article, "The Job Blahs: Who Wants to Work?" *Newsweek* analyzes the growing force of alienated workers who are bored, rebellious, or frustrated about their jobs. The mood of this vast segment of blue-collar and white-collar workers affects not only the nation's productivity but more importantly the individual worker's sense of himself.[11]

The problem is that the old ethic does not fit the needs of today's social and economic conditions. New work patterns created by automation, cybernetics, electronics, and information processing have changed the picture. We are told that "within 25 years, two per cent of our population working in the factory and on the farm will be able to produce all the goods and food needed by the other 98 per cent."[12] In fact, we have already become a service society "now that we have more people engaged in producing services than in producing goods."[13]

Consequently, there are new problems attendant to unemployment, work alienation, and job retraining. No longer is there the one-to-one relationship between the worker and the finished product. The technological revolution has abolished scarcity and has made many kinds of work unfulfilling or even unnecessary.

In the search for providing job enrichment, some employers today are making possible greater flexibility in work requirements for their employees. In Sweden the Volvo and Saab auto manufacturers recently decided to break up the assembly line and work instead with assembly teams. General Motors is experimenting with a team approach to the assembly of its new $13,000 motor home. Some electronic firms have switched to unit production in order to provide closer identification with the finished product. Polaroid has tried job rotation and also has permitted employees to organize their own work. Several West German firms have inaugurated the gliding workday, permitting employees to set their work hours as they like within limits. There has been some experimentation with granting employees the privilege of choosing their workdays out of the week. Sabbaticals with full pay, the extended weekend, and other plans for cross-fertilization of ideas and experience have been tried to enhance job satisfaction and fight the malaise of boredom because of meaningless work assignments.[14]

To what extent have our attitudes and beliefs been influenced by the traditional work ethic? Furthermore, how do its fundamental ideas measure up when tested against Christian principles? These questions can be approached through a scrutiny of the various doctrines in the American business creed as presented earlier from Rasmussen's work.

Individualism

Rugged individualism has been one of the primary motifs of American life. The frontier was dotted by men and women who bravely conquered it alone. They could rightly take the credit for their efforts and successes; if there was hard luck or misfortune, they could likewise take that "on the chin." In the development of American industry there are countless episodes of individuals who in the Horatio Alger tradition fought their way from poverty to financial success.

These kinds of success stories are still common among us. Rugged individualism is a norm which demands respect. It grows out of a notion that individuals have their own ironclad inner characteristics and can excel in spite of all odds.

While in a valid sense Protestantism is individualistic in that every man stands in responsibility before God, the biblical view always sees the human individual as encountering God's will in the context of time and place and as a member of a covenant people. Economic life, no less than the life of worship, is lived under God and with His people. The Christian view about economic life at this point would recognize that man is in fact an interactive creature, responding and being responded to; negotiating, trading, and bargaining not only in economic goods but also in the areas of ideas, beliefs, and appreciations.[15]

Self-Reliance

Closely associated with individualism is the honored virtue of self-reliance. Although some might credit the maxim "God helps those who help themselves" to the Bible, it is actually attributed to Algernon Sidney (1622-1683) and quoted by Benjamin Franklin. The individual who by sheer pluck and determination rises from humble beginnings to power and wealth describes a hero in our culture. The cult of the self-made man has been popular in America, although President Lincoln said you could always pick them out because they were made so poorly.

However, in the efficient business organizations of today the self-reliant individualist is a dying breed. He does not fit well into the mold of the "organization man." Rasmussen claims that the tenet of self-reliance "is obviously unrealistic concerning all men, and particularly in an increasingly interdependent society where single individuals are almost totally impotent unless they work in and through large organizations which coordinate the work of large numbers of individuals."[16] From the Christian standpoint any mood of self-sufficiency must be tempered by the acknowledgment of our dependence upon God for our very existence and the unavoidable contacts with Him in every decision in life. Likewise we must acknowledge the help and interaction of the brotherhood in decision-making.

Productivity

The American business creed holds that the volume of material produced is the chief measure of economic well-being. It presupposes an endless supply of raw material and a limitless market for goods. We gauge our national health in terms of G.N.P. (gross national product), emphasizing is quantity rather than quality.

A Christian is compelled to be concerned with fairer distribution, as well as increased productivity. He recognizes that material affluence tends to blind his eyes to the total needs of man and dull his sense of dependence upon God. A Christian demands a more realistic concept of human welfare than is provided merely by data on income and output. A British economist argues "that a materialistic society interested primarily in piling up more and more material goods is destructive of humane values and is in pursuit of goals contrary to human happiness."[17]

Activism

Americans have traditionally worshiped the activist principle. This mood lies at the heart of the traditional work ethic which prescribed work not only as an antidote for idleness but also as the center for all human activity. We admire the man of action who gets things done. There is a great emphasis on activism in our Christian faith. Our religion is one of verbs: acting, responding, loving, witnessing, serving. Man is an active and interactive being.

Even though our theology is on the side of activity we dare not honor activity for its own sake. To what purpose or what end do we act? What is the quality of our activity? Is it kingdom advancing, neutral, or detrimental? How do we balance input and output in our lives? From the theological perspective what is involved in the relationship between God who acts and man who responds?

Progress and optimism

Faith in human progress and an unbounding optimism about human endeavor have been characteristic of secular thinking in Western culture. In America we have turned progress into a kind of national religion especially as it relates to our material standard of living. We are committed to ideas of change and progress. We are willing to be temporarily inconvenienced, for the sake of anticipated advancement.

John A. Kouwenhoven[18] in an article entitled "What's American about America?" refers to a "progress morality" which he describes as the principle of the "infinitely extendible." We lay out streets in grid patterns which are infinitely extendible. We finish off skyscrapers not with towers, peak roofs, or cornices to provide a climax, but rather with a clean stoppage of construction at a certain point as though the building might be infinitely extendible upward.

Christian optimism is based on trust in God, not in the sure and inevitable progress of history nor in the confidence that man's efforts can alone solve his perennial problems. Christian hope lies secure only in God's hands. He is the initiator; we the respondents. Confession and the ability for self-criticism by the grace of God are important for growth toward more responsible life and witness.[19]

Competition

Central to the American business way has been the concept of free competition. In earlier times when competition was relatively unregulated it often became cutthroat in effect. The strong prevailed and the weak and small, lacking power to resist for long the advance of big business, were soon swallowed up by their larger competitors. Competition has been referred to as "the life of the trade." Positively it promotes improved quality of goods and helps to keep control in pricing.

Competition raises some difficult ethical questions: Is competition a characteristic of human nature? Is it an expression of selfishness? To what extent is it culturally conditioned? How well has it worked as an economic regulator? Are all interests served fairly by the competitive system? These are crucial issues to be worked out by those who can responsibly combine economic and ethical considerations.

Consumer sovereignty

The classical business creed claimed that the consumer is king and makes the basic decisions governing what is produced in the economy by acceptance or rejection on the market. This tenet has the effect of relieving the producer from moral judgments as to what is good or bad for others. He simply offers the goods or services and leaves it to the consumer to cast the vote as to what should dominate the culture. The consumer may or may not be able to handle such decisions responsibly.

In actual practice there is evidence that consumer sovereignty does not work too effectively in an increasingly complex economy. It is virtually impossible for the consumer to get all the facts he ought to have, since it's the business of the multibillion dollar advertising industry to mold his judgment. It seems evident that modern advertising and marketing techniques are geared to influence consumer spending more to the benefit of the producers than to match what is necessarily good for the consumer. Note the resistance, and support, given to Ralph Nader in his efforts for consumer welfare.

Self-interest

The profit motive, a universal characteristic of economic life, must be recognized in both ethical and practical considerations. Self-interest lies behind the efforts which men are willing to expend for a project or a cause. It is important to acknowledge this motivation in human endeavor.

Several ethical considerations must be noted concern-

A Critical Look at the Traditional Work Ethic

ing the motivation of self-interest, no matter how enlightened its claims. The profit motive without some measure of accountability is folly. There are many examples of men who became exploitive, taking maximum advantage of others in every transaction. This kind of preoccupation is in the end destructive of self.

Christ's claims upon His followers act as proper restraints upon self-interest. He would save us from the kind of selfishness that leads to self-deception and defensiveness. Self-interest can never be a glorious virtue in its own right but must always be subjected to a cause beyond oneself. Christ would give us the capacity for self-criticism and self-transcendence, so that we can direct self-interest into constructive channels and submit it to transformation and restraint.[20]

Rasmussen offers some helpful remarks in relating the tenet of self-interest to the corporate establishment.

> Self-interest always is dangerously compounded when operating in powerful organizations. It is easier for a General Motors man to believe that what is good for GM is good for the nation than it is to believe that what is good for me is good for you. When large groups celebrate their loyalty and common identification, it becomes a kind of narrow patriotism under which disloyalty reaps corporate scorn and disapproval. The big bureaucracy tends to develop yes-men who show enthusiasm in expediting the standard policy and moralizing its legitimacy in order to gain advancement.[21]

In summary, what principles should a Christian take with him in the realm of economic decision-making?

Albert T. Rasmussen suggests two basic considerations which guide Christian thought on economic matters. One is the basic recognition of the supremacy of persons over things. Persons are not tools nor should they be reduced to exploitable resources. The second is the recognition of the significance of community as the supporting context for one's personal life and conduct. It is the responsibility of Christians and the church to make corporate judgments about the great issues of economic responsibility as the Holy Spirit leads and corrects us.[22]

10. Christian Vocation, Work, and Job

The meaning of man's work is the satisfaction of the instinct for adventure that God has implanted in his heart —
Paul Tournier

A Christian work ethic which befits a post-industrial age demands a reexamination of the concepts of vocation and work. In the historical survey we have noted the medieval view that put labor into sacred and secular compartments, the Reformation doctrine that made of all work a divine calling, and the secularized notion that idolized work for its own sake. However, none of these views adequately fits an era of changing balance between work and leisure time. Regardless of whether advancing leisure is accepted as an option by choice or a reality forced upon us by changing social conditions, a new perspective is needed for the ethic of work in the coming decades.

The undergirding work principle remains the

same; its applications must be adjusted to fit changing social situations. The biblical work ordinance recognizes the creative purpose of God. Man is to replenish the earth, subdue it, and have dominion over all other living things. While modern technical devices have lifted the burden of toil, it is still true that work — manual, mental, or spiritual — is a fact of our existence. The preacher of Ecclesiastes romanticized the fact and benefits of work as a gift from God. "There is nothing better for a man than that he should eat and drink, and find enjoyment in his toil. This also, I saw, is from the hand of God; for apart from him who can eat or who can have enjoyment?" [1]

Vocation and work

The *Bible* is the story of God and His people. God called out persons to be His instruments in fulfilling His redemptive purposes for men. The stage was set when God called Abram to leave Haran and to go out to a place he was to receive as an inheritance. By faith he obeyed and followed. W. R. Forrester says of Abraham, "He was the first man with a definite, explicit sense of vocation." [2]

Within this new nation called by God, various individuals were singled out for special duties such as priests, prophets, kings, artisans, or craftsmen. In Exodus 31 the Lord told Moses, "I have called by name Bezaleel . . . and I have filled him with the spirit of God, in wisdom, and in understanding, and in knowledge . . . to work in all manner of workmanship." [3]

Christian Vocation, Work, and Job 113

In formulating a Christian ethic of work, Virgil Vogt in *The Christian Calling* reminds us that the starting point, just as it was for Abraham, is with the call of God. We are called to forsake all and follow Christ. Acceptance of the Christian vocation means to acknowledge the primary claims of Christ and to reorder one's life accordingly. Life has been given a new goal. A Christian is in the service of God to be a bearer of love and a servant to his neighbor. This call of faith concerns all of life and its activities. [4]

New Testament scholars disagree as to whether the "calling" ever refers in the Scriptures to "occupation" or "work in life." Alan Richardson in *The Biblical Doctrine of Work* defends the position that the Christian calling or vocation always refers to that act of God whereby He summons men into the kingdom. He says,

> The Bible knows no instance of a man's being called to an earthly profession or trade by God. St. Paul, for example, is called to be an apostle; he is not called to be a tent-maker. . . . We cannot with propriety speak of God's calling a man to be an engineer or a doctor or a schoolmaster. God calls doctors and engineers and school masters to be prophets, evangelists, pastors and teachers as laymen in his Church. . . . Our secular occupations are to be regarded not as ends in themselves but as means to the service of the Kingdom of God. [5]

A contrasting view is taken by Wade H. Boggs, Jr., in his book, *All Ye That Labor*. He refers in particular to the words of Paul in 1 Corinthians, "Let every man abide in the same calling wherein he was called." [6]

Boggs notes that the Greek stem for "calling" is used in two different senses in this verse. The second is the usual New Testament meaning of the summons into the kingdom while the first is defined by the context as meaning one's station or status in life. The effect of this interpretation is to imply "that the social or professional situation of the individual Christian should become his vocation, that it should be regarded as the state or condition which the Lord has assigned to him."[7] This view seems to be a restatement of the Protestant work ethic which related calling and work.

In light of the changing role of work in our society this discussion shall make a distinction between a Christian's vocation and his work. The Christian vocation is to be a follower of Christ, a bearer of love and a servant to his neighbor. This is the commitment to which he directs his very being. The Christian vocation is the privilege and duty of all who have responded affirmatively to the gracious call of God.

Work or occupation, then, may be defined as that undertaking for which one prepares and through which one accomplishes or produces that which is humanly meaningful. It involves the exercise of human capacities and a display of judgment, style, or sense of craft. It yields some stable accomplishments to which one can point as the product of his effort. A person may be a storekeeper, farmer, factory worker, or teacher.[8]

In themselves these forms of work ought not be sacralized with the claims of divine call. Both Christians and non-Christians find their employ in these and similar occupations. Work, per se, must be considered as ethically neutral or amoral. Ethical judgments about work need to be made on the basis of such considerations as its motivations, its stewardship values, and its regard for human and ecological concerns. The important questions are how and why work is performed.

Work and job

Thomas F. Green of Syracuse University suggests an interesting reinterpretation of the Protestant work ethic as it applies to a Christian's view of work today. He notes "that what is significant about the Reformation view is not the fact that it related work and calling, but that in so doing it united work and job." [9] The Protestant ethic gave to every job an intrinsic value and made of it a religious duty.

Consequently, Green suggests that in addition to the former distinctions made between vocation and work we should also differentiate work and job. As noted previously work refers to one's chosen occupation or profession. A job describes what is done for remuneration, a way of earning a living, the more temporary occupational use of time. It is associated with a particular place, group of associates, and kind of activity or responsibility. A Christian in the profession of teaching, for instance, holds a job at a particular school and in responsibility for a particular group of students.

While the Christian vocation is a life commitment and one's work is a long-term association by reason of training, interest, identification, and experience, a job implies the more flexible nature of one's gainful employ. The average American holds six different jobs in his lifetime.

In differentiating vocation, work, and job it should be emphasized that the priorities set up due to the Christian calling will affect one's work and job. One's vocation permeates all of life. Therefore, a Christian chooses the kind of work through which he can express his calling. He rejects a work which would compromise or conflict with his faith commitment. Likewise, one's work and job may and often do overlap or indeed may be coterminous. This makes for a happy combination because it implies that the job is one with meaning and satisfaction.

The job, however, may be one which is simply endured for the sake of making a living. This may describe many jobs today in which the employee feels an alienation with respect to his work. Because the job is associated with endless repetition and drudgery, he complains that it is not meaningful. Such a job should not be made to carry the psychological freight of being responsible for a sense of personal worth. Identification with a life interest should not be forced upon such a job. Green says, "It is often our jobs that make it possible for us to do our work; at the same time it is often our work that makes a job bearable and as attractive as it is. In neither case should one's job be confused with one's work, with the result of taking the job too seriously."[10]

A Christian's work

The Christian work ethic would minimize the tendency to rank work in a kind of hierarchy of importance. In subtle and not so subtle ways we leave the impression that at the top, for earnest Christians, are placed the ordained ministry and missionary service. Closely allied to these are occupations with a distinctly "human" content, such as education, medicine, and social service. Many of the professions are commonly thought of as affording opportunity for the fulfillment of a genuinely Christian vocation. Farming, perhaps, comes in the same category. Then there is a vast range of industrial and service occupations that are apt to be thought of as religiously neutral.

This kind of thinking, stated or implied, has its roots in the medieval view of the two orders. It is subject to dangers because it denies the claims of the Christian calling upon all followers. It tends to make the distinctive and primary interest of the church the end rather than the means of serving the total needs of men's lives. It is true that there are activities in modern society whose effects bring harm to man rather than good. In these a Christian should have no part. But any work in which a contribution can be made somewhere to the total needs of man must be regarded as a good and natural way for a Christian to live his calling. To attempt to place any work or occupation in a special category is to limit the meaning of Christian vocation.[11]

It is reasonable to believe that our work as Christians should be performed well. If I am a teacher, I should be a good teacher; and if a farmer, a good farmer. Divine calling somehow modifies and enlarges our work so that it is not the same as a non-Christian engaged in a similar occupation. The life of Christ is a good example. While He probably devoted some years to the work of a carpenter and was no doubt a good carpenter, His calling was "to preach good news to the poor . . . to proclaim release to the captives and recovering of sight to the blind, to set at liberty those who are oppressed, and to proclaim the acceptable year of the Lord."[12] This calling He took up seriously following His baptism. Christ set the example by performing His work in perfect harmony with the fulfillment of His calling. In the Christian view this is work at its best.

Work for a Christian is inseparable from service to our fellowman. This belief about work grows out of a view of man as existing not in individual isolation but in community and in responsibility to his neighbor. A Christian's occupation should be one in which society is truly served. This would exclude all endeavors in which the end product would be harmful in any way.

From the standpoint of the employer it means that man as worker cannot be separated from man as person. A primary aim of industry in setting up means for efficient production is the provision for the kind of climate where individuals and groups realize maximum satisfactions in their work.[13]

The true product of work is meaning. Unlike the paycheck, meaning cannot be earned. It is a gift depending both on the worker and his work. Colossians 3:22-24 in the Phillips translation says:

> Your job is to obey your [employer], not with the idea of currying favor, but as a sincere expression of your devotion to the Lord. Whatever you do, put your whole heart and soul into it, as into work done for the Lord, and not merely for men — knowing that your real reward, a heavenly one, will come from the Lord, since

you are actually employed by the Lord Christ and not just by your earthly [employer].[14]

One who follows Christ in daily life works ultimately for God. He works not only for what he gets in return but primarily because of who he is. As a representative of Christ he knows the satisfaction which comes from helping others. His deeds are acts of service for God.

In the final analysis the essence of man lies not in what he does, but in what he is. Thus the Christian must draw a distinction between himself and his work. The criterion for work is doing, not being. There is no possibility of intrinsic self-worth in work. Man, in the Christian view, must not treat himself simply as a tool, nor find his truest self-estimation upon what he has accomplished. Rather, his worth is bound up in who and what he is, in his faith relationship to Christ as Savior and Lord. In the spiritual sense our standing is in Christ.

> For by grace are ye saved through faith; and that not of yourselves: it is the gift of God: not of works, lest any man should boast. For we are his workmanship, created in Christ Jesus unto good works, which God hath before ordained that we should walk in them.[15]

Leisure and work

This distinction between work and job offers some solution to the dilemma of the future when the production of goods and services will take the labor of only a small percentage of available manpower. Some even foresee the day when a part of the population may be on a guaranteed income because there aren't enough jobs to go around. In any case, job time will continue to decrease with a corresponding increase of free time. If a man's job can be distinguished from his work he can then accept a routine job if necessary (or even a guaranteed income) as a way of making a living but look to a broader context for the meaning of work in his life. His challenge will be to discover a work to do, a lifetime career which may or may not coincide with the particular job he has at the moment. Work will be a thing he lives to do, rather than a thing he does to live.

Although it would help to make jobs more meaningful, the real problem is for more people to discover a work to be accomplished. . . . There is a tremendous gulf between the man who views his career, in retrospect, as the succession of jobs that he has held and the man who views his career, in prospect, as something that is to be accomplished by him.[16]

Might this suggest an area in which leisure may perform a distinct function in the future? Through leisure man may discover the opportunities and possibilities for a work which expresses human creativity and initiative. Through leisure he may find that sense of meaning, that hope of accomplishment, that self-identity which brings wholeness to life. Through leisure he may be directed to the kinds of creative accomplishment which add up to a satisfying lifework.[17]

IV. In Praise of Leisure -- The Leisure Ethic

11. God's People and Leisure

Work is the main course, the meat and substance of our lives. Recreation is the dessert: we like it best in modest portions at the end of a good meal. When we try to substitute the dessert for the meal itself, we lose our taste for it. — *John Luther*

In biblical times the concept of leisure as we know it today did not exist. The possibility of full economic production with time left over was an unheard-of dream. Therefore, the specific characteristics which make for leisure in an industrial age were simply not present. In any such early agrarian society the most that can be said for leisure is that work was interrupted by occasional time-out and rest periods. One leisure authority described the pattern thus:

> The working year followed a timetable written in the very passage of the days and seasons; in good weather work was hard, in bad weather, it slackened off. Work of this kind had a natural rhythm to it, punctuated by rests, songs, games, and ceremonies.[1]

In the absence of leisure in the modern sense the Bible says little about how free time should be used. It is obvious that the work motif was central. However, according to the command of God it is also clear that both work and rest were to be woven into the life of His people. "six days thou shalt do thy work, and on the seventh day thou shalt rest: that thine ox and thine ass may rest, and the son of thy handmaid, and the stranger, may be refreshed."[2]

The rest principle

Sabbath rest was enjoined by the law of Moses and the day was to be strictly observed as blessed and hallowed by God. Worship was the primary motive for the day of rest. Work was put aside; travel and commercial transactions were prohibited. Even the necessary food was to be prepared the day before. Since the Sabbath was a holy day it gave purpose and meaning to the whole of time. It was to be a joyous day in appreciation for the privilege of worshiping God.[3]

The rest principle also found application in the practice of a sabbatical year, the one in seven when even the land was to lie fallow. After the space of seven sabbaths of years, or 49 years, there came on the fiftieth year a special celebration of jubilee. Land and possessions were redeemed by the original owners and special religious observances were provided. The sabbatical principle carried with it a definite social welfare function. Furthermore, God provided for the physical needs of the rest year through an extra bountiful harvest in the preceding year.[4]

Early in biblical history a cycle of special religious

days began to develop; some days for feasting and festivity, others for fasting and penance. In either case work was taboo as the Israelites acknowledged or celebrated God's care for them. The connection between rest and worship was well established.

One such God-ordained vacation, the Feast of the Tabernacles, is described in Nehemiah 8. The participants were expected to build little booths and to leave their homes to live in these for a week's time. This occasion combined spiritual renewal, feasting, and gladness. The Book of the Law was read each day. A unique element was the family shared experience.

The rhythm of work and rest was exemplified further in the life of Christ. It was, however, more an alternating of an active ministry with an intense devotional life. Christ often chose to occupy His free time in prayer and meditation. He frequently made retreats either alone or with His disciples in order to refresh Himself physically and spiritually. Prayer, meditation, and fellowship were Christ's prime leisure activities.[5]

Holy days and holidays

The Christians in the first century reduced the number of holy days inherited from Judaism and reinterpreted them in light of their new faith. One significant change was the transition from the Sabbath to the observance of Sunday. The day of rest which formerly had followed six days of toil now became the first day of the week in celebration of the Christ event.

No other ancient peoples developed a day each week exclusively for religious pursuits as did the Hebrews. The Romans set aside a series of days honoring their gods and these "holy days" became the basis for the term "holiday" which we use today. These occasions which originally held ceremonial meaning tended to become times when the primary observance was freedom from the requirements of work. Robert Lee points out that "Greek celebrations finally reached the place where feast days outnumbered working days; and Roman holidays with their games grew to 135 days a year in the second century and then to 175 in the fourth century."[6]

In the Middle Ages the character of leisure was influenced by the divine sanction which the church had ascribed to work. In effect, God's work and rest were one; so it was to be for all who had experienced the grace of God. John Preston Dever notes that "St. Augustine established an active leisure based on the tranquility of action in Christ. Through this active rest love became the transcending power of one's life and one experienced the eternal Sabbath or the heavenly existence on earth."[7] In practical terms good works were to fill leisure time in order for man to escape the natural desires of his body. The medieval church was skeptical about any kind of pleasure which might lead to the arousal of sexual desires.

As long as monasticism held the day, idleness was strongly condemned. However, as Robert Lee notes, a host of holy days was again added to the calendar by the church. In fact nonwork time accumulated to the point that it became a question whether the net effect was primarily that of providing for leisure and worship or of creating conditions of idleness and economic impoverishment. Actually, it was some of both. In any case the church condemned the characteristic riotous and drunken behavior of feast days and urged a more pious morality.[8]

St. Thomas Aquinas (1225-1274), who set as his life task the reconciliation of Aristotle's thought and the Christian faith, brought together the classical view of leisure and the medieval practice of the contemplative life. Aquinas regarded the contemplative life as superior to the active life. He would not even consider the life of pleasure because that was the life of a beast and not of man.[9]

As noted earlier Luther's doctrine of vocation was the first definite break from a dualistic view of work. Luther extended equality before God to the working man as well as to the monk in the cloister. All of life was sacred. This had tremendous implications for leisure. Every honorable activity of man, including his free time, could be used creatively to the glory of God. It is doubtful, however, whether Luther realized what this meant in terms of sanctifying leisure time. Luther continued to find time to drink with his friends and to discuss theology.[10]

John Calvin moved toward a more realistic attitude about leisure urging the moderate use of all time. He opposed excesses but approved of moderation in the arts, games, and social practices of the day. For instance, Calvin was not opposed to the use of leisure time for drinking wine and having fellowship, as long as it was kept in check and contributed to the rhythm of life. Unfortunately, his followers missed his call for moderation and made of his teachings a basis for worldly asceticism and a distrust of all impulsive pleasures.

With the influence of these Protestant Reformers and their followers there came another cutback on the number of holy days on the grounds of economic necessity and of holiday misuse.[11]

On the New England shores the Puritans continued the revolt against excesses of holy days. With their emphasis on the virtues of austerity and hard work they distrusted the ostentations of ceremonial occasions. Rather, they sought a more simple and ascetic religious expression. Furthermore, many of the holidays were tied to traditions of the mother country and thus were inappropriate to the new land. Perhaps the greatest influence was simply the necessity of hard work and the scarcity of time left over for celebration.

In subsequent American history the trend has been reversed once more with the provision of added days to celebrate our religious, national, and cultural heritage. To the various religious and patriotic holidays has been added a host of special days: seasonal (New Year's Day, May Day), family (Mother's Day, Father's Day) ethnic (St. Patrick's Day for the Irish, Columbus Day for the Italians), organizational (founders' days and anniversaries), plus countless weeks of special emphases (Secretaries Week, Brotherhood Week). Furthermore, by federal law passed in 1971 five holidays not ordinarily falling over a weekend were made part of three-day weekends, in order to provide better utilization of the holidays for leisure purposes.

The celebration of holy days and holidays is only one measure in the total development of leisure. A more complete analysis of leisure patterns might examine the development of the arts and crafts, communication and travel, play activities, social conventions, and other aspects of the culture. Suffice it to say that while the idea of leisure as we know it today has roots in the biblical principle of work and rest, the Greek concept of leisure, and the medieval practice of contemplation, it finds its truest expression in modern industrial society.

Before leisure can become possible in the life of the masses of people two conditions must be present according to Dumazedier. These conditions exist only in a society permeated by the urban values of industrialization. First, the society ceases to govern its activities by means of common ritual obligations, such as feasts and holy days. Rather, work and leisure become an individual responsibility even though one's choices may still be influenced by social necessity. Second, there is a clear and arbitrary differentiation between work and leisure. They are separated not only in theory and practice but also tend to reflect competitive values.[12]

The prerequisite conditions for leisure about which Dumazedier refers have become a fact in American society within the past several generations. The pursuit of leisure is considered to be an individual matter; work and leisure values tend to be in conflict rather than in support of each other. New kinds of work have replaced former rural pursuits, thus opening up new leisure possibilities and problems.

Leisure practices in the Mennonite Church

The Christian community has felt the effects of this change no less than the broader American society.

An illustration of this shift of values is drawn from the Mennonites whose long tradition of rural life is being replaced by urbanized work and leisure patterns today. J. C. Wenger describes the following scene as typical of a Mennonite family a century ago:

> One hundred years ago the typical Mennonite family had little occasion for recreation in any formal sense and perhaps still less opportunity. Father rose daily at 4:00 a.m. to get the cows milked before going to the fields for the day. Mother had to arise early to prepare a steaming breakfast for her large family. The older boys helped their father, and the girls their mother. Grass was cut with scythes, and grain with a cradle. Grain was shocked by hand, and threshed with a flail. There were no milking machines, no corn pickers, no binders or combines — indeed no labor-saving machinery at all. People toiled from early dawn to late at night to wrest a living from the soil. On Sundays the young men gathered at the farm of one of the members of the church and played corner ball, and during the long winter evenings simple games like figmill were played by the children of the family. The human desire for play was not to be totally suppressed, so there was lots of fun mixed into the monotonous work of the day. Young men played pranks on one another, of course, and as lines of men would whet their scythes together they would chant:
>
> > Der Wetz iss gut, der Wetz iss gut;
> > Der Hinnerscht hat'n Schlang im Hut!
>
> (The sharpening is going fine, going fine;
> A snake's in the hat of the last one in line!)
>
> There was also some horseplay at Halloween, and unfortunately in many communities the young men used to gather at taverns for a social evening of fellowship. (Young

God's People and Leisure

people in the nineteenth century typically waited until after marriage to turn to the Lord and unite with the church.) Moving pictures had not been invented and there was no radio or television. The recreation problem of the young people was not even recognized as existing. It was simply taken for granted that *junges Blut hat viel Muth* (Young blood has lots of life), and the young people would in due time settle down and establish homes.[13]

At the beginning of the present century most Mennonites lived and worked on the farm. They, like many others, valued hard work and industriousness and avoided recreation and play. The approach to leisure activities was primarily negative. Participation in games and sports was opposed because of the associations with the patterns and passions of the world. Mennonite historian Melvin Gingerich says that "since 1865 more than 120 conference resolutions defining and condemning worldly amusements have been passed by the various Mennonite district conferences."[14]

Historically, a genuine concern for the spirituality of its people led the church to warn against "worldly amusements." Of course, a strong adherence to the work ethic is recognized as an important factor too. Manual labor and hard work were honorable and led to true satisfactions. Play for adults was thought to be a waste of time and therefore of little profit. Only for children could play be legitimately justified.

Evan Oswald in an analysis of recreational trends in the Mennonite Church noted that denominational attitudes toward recreational activities have passed through an historical progression from opposition to toleration to acceptance in the last one hundred years.[15] Much of this change has been influenced by the general economic and social trends in American society affecting work and leisure patterns. No longer are corn-huskings, quilting bees, barn-raisings, and other forms of cooperative activity a recreational option for most people. No longer are the majority of Mennonites following the traditional lifestyles of the rural community. No longer are Mennonites isolated from the recreational activities and facilities of public education, parks, playgrounds, and commercialized amusements.

Oswald summarized the current Mennonite acceptance of leisure activities as follows:

> Today the Mennonite people are acepting recreational activities as vital to wholesome Christian living. The Mennonite rural patterns of living are being strongly influenced by urban culture. Rural types of recreation have largely been replaced by urban types. Farm mechanization, prosperity, and more leisure time have ushered in the need for, desire for, and practice of recreational pursuits. Opposition to recreation and sports participation is rapidly being replaced by camping programs, vacation trips, church leagues, promotional work by the Commission for Christian Education, and by recreation promotion articles in church periodicals.
>
> Mennonite Church leaders are no longer giving only passive sanction to the recreational activities of the church's young people. They are calling for recreational programs to meet personal needs, home needs, and church needs. They are calling for church leadership and guidance in recreational programming and promotion. Their call for recreational activities and programs is consistently qualified with the appeal that all recreational pursuits should be Christ-centered in purpose, practice, and outcome.[16]

12. *In Praise of Leisure*

Leisure can be a real friend if you know how to use it; a formidable enemy if you abuse it. — *Thomas G. Desmond*

In developing the historical patterns of leisure it was noted that the leisure concept had its early beginnings in Greek culture and later found adaptation in the contemplative life of the medieval monks. With the strong influence of the Protestant work ethic, leisure was relegated in practice to a position outside the church. Only in recent years has the church again looked at the matter, seeking to come to terms with leisure and its possibilities.

In searching for an ethic of leisure scholars have used various theological bases: the doctrine of creation, of time, of man, of the church, of vocation, or of revelation. Pioneer work on the theology of leisure was done by Josef Pieper in *Leisure, the Basis of Culture,* by suggesting that we need to set aside the prejudice that comes from overvaluating the sphere of work. Differentiating leisure from "Acadia," the deadly sin of sloth, Pieper approaches leisure in a positive manner. Real leisure is a divine time for celebration, commemorated at its best in feast and holy days.[1]

Robert Lee's important study on leisure was commissioned by the Leisure Time Witness Study Committee of the National Council of Churches in 1954. His book, *Religion and Leisure in America,* develops the Christian doctrine of time. Lee shows how man's time and God's eternity relate in the Christian's use of leisure.[2]

In a recent book entitled *The Christian Encounters the New Leisure* Rudolf F. Norden bases his argument on the Christian doctrine of vocation.[3] As part of Christian vocation God calls His followers to leisure alongside His call to work. Joseph H. Gates sees leisure as integral in God's creative activity[4]; Harvey Cox ties leisure to the function of the servant church.[5]

We shall investigate further some of the theological assumptions which relate to leisure and which help us understand the acceptance and concern of the church regarding the new leisure.

Leisure as God's gift, bound up in the creation model

> In the beginning God created the heaven and the earth. . . . And God saw every thing that he had made, and, behold, it was very good. And the evening and the morning were the sixth day. . . . And on the seventh day God ended his work which he had made; and he rested on the seventh day from all his work. . . . And God blessed the seventh day, and sanctified it.[6]

God existed before all things and it was He who

set the universe in motion. After six days of creative work He rested from His labors. Reflecting upon what had been accomplished He declared that it was very good. The seventh day, the one marked for rest, was a sign of freedom within the whole creative cycle. The Ruler of Creation was free to stand apart, to catch His breath, to reflect, and to enjoy a new perspective on what He had done. The act of rest completed God's creative accomplishment. "For in six days the Lord made heaven and earth, and on the seventh day he rested, and was refreshed."[7]

We need to see the wholeness of the creative act, which includes both work and leisure. Joseph H. Gates says, "God created the earth, and its creatures, and man, not for His work, but for His leisure. Creation itself was (and is) an act of 'work' but also of God's creative, leisure activity."[8] This truth of creation sets our lives, our work, and our leisure (rest) into a context of human fulfillment and re-creative possibility.

Based on the creation model, God commanded His people through Moses: "Six days thou shalt labour, and do all thy work: but the seventh day is the sabbath of the Lord thy God: in it thou shalt not do any work. . . . wherefore the Lord blessed the sabbath day, and hallowed it."[9] Originally, man had been placed in the Garden of Eden to dress and keep it. But with the transgression, work became the measure of man's activity and the meaning of true leisure was marred. Thus man needed to be reminded of the purpose and sanctity of the one day of rest.

Christ reaffirmed this principle of rest in His rebuke of the Pharisees who kept the letter of the Sabbath but lost its spirit. Because they complained about the disciples who plucked grain to eat as they went through the fields on the Sabbath, Jesus declared, "The sabbath was made for man, and not man for the sabbath: therefore the Son of man is Lord also of the sabbath."[10] Man's fulfillment is not to be completely identified with work. "Man's work, like his Creator's is crowned with his rest, and his chief end is not to labor but to enjoy God forever."[11]

On another occasion Christ reminded His followers that there is a time to rest — a time to learn of God. His gracious invitation is addressed to all people. "Come unto me, all ye that labour and are heavy laden, and I will give you rest. Take my yoke upon you, and learn of me; for I am meek and lowly in heart: and ye shall find rest unto your souls."[12] While it is important to rest physically from work, it is more important to find our rest, our dependence, in God.

Robert Lee emphasizes this ongoing continuous essence of creativity. We share in creation, he says, not in the sense of God who created something out of nothing, but in the sense that we as intelligent creatures can re-create, rearrange, and bring forth new relationships out of the basic elements already existing. Our talents, resourcefulness, and imagination are at God's disposal for His new creation within our lives. Day-by-day re-creation implies refurbishing and refitting tired muscles, frayed nerves, and weary brain cells for new and continued service. In its fullest expression man's re-creative activity relates him to the Creator of all things.[13]

Leisure as an expression of the lordship of Christ over all of life

A Christian knows who he is. Through accepting the gracious invitation of God to forsake sin and his evil ways he has found his life and values turned around in a new faith relationship with Christ. He is a follower and a servant, God's person in the world.

Since Christ is Lord over all of a Christian's life, as His followers we are called to glorify God both in our work and leisure. We dare not dichotomize life, as though it is necessary to honor God with our work but when leisure time comes we have somehow earned the freedom to make our own choices as if God doesn't matter. This would be missing the real meaning of God's rule in our lives. The totality of our commitment to Christ knows no off-bounds areas of time or of activity. Under the lordship of Christ any attempt to fragment work or leisure as being outside the will of God fades away.

While leisure implies a certain freedom and non-obligation this does not place our free time outside the context of responsibility to God for all of life. Rather, increased leisure time adds to the possibility and task of having leisure to the glory of God. To live abundantly places all time and activities under His sovereignty.

Throughout history, man has tended to exalt one aspect of life at the expense of another — meditation, amusement, work, or leisure. Work has monopolized the last three centuries. The restoration of leisure in a balanced role is a move toward the recognition of Christ's lordship over the totality of life.

Leisure as the sharing and participating use of God's gift of time

The Christian lives in time. His time has value and significance because it is a gift from God. Since work and leisure make up the bulk of most people's waking hours, these are the segments of time which demand attention. Actually it is better to look at these not as separate functions to be performed but rather as a rhythm of life to be lived. In God's gift of time we both toil and rest, contemplate and act, produce and consume, give and take, accept and share, serve and receive, work and have leisure.

Time brings a responsibility. Twice in the New Testament we are told to "redeem the time"[14] indicating that it is precious and can be squandered. Consequently we need to choose those leisure activities which contribute meaning and purpose to our lives. Leisure becomes a challenge and an opportunity rather than time that is left over to squander or kill. The question of leisure-time activities calls us to the commitment of being true stewards of all of God's gift of time.

We are given a scriptural criterion by which to test our use of time. "And whatsoever ye do in word or deed, do all in the name of the Lord Jesus, giving thanks to God and the Father by him."[15] Just as God appraised His creative activities we need to examine our use of time. Time is to be taken seriously. "Leisure is not empty time, but it should be fulfilled, redeemed, and responsible time."[16]

The significance of time has to do ultimately with the quality of events in our experience. The worth of leisure time has to do with such intangibles as its

In Praise of Leisure

richness, its awareness, its sensitivity, its wonder, and its challenge. These stand in opposition to the kinds of pastime activities which yield boredom, alienation, distractions, and tension. For the Christian "there is the assurance that God, as revealed in Jesus Christ, desires that we enjoy an abundant life — not solely in terms of wealth and things, but in terms of rich experiences, mutual help and sacrifice, and faithfulness to him and to our fellows."[17]

Two verses from a poem by Michel Quoist contrast the basic attitudes about time:

> Good-bye, Sir, I haven't time.
> I'll come back, I can't wait, I haven't time.
> I must end this letter — I haven't time.
> I'd love to help you, but I haven't time.
> I can't accept, having no time.
> I can't think, I can't read, I'm swamped, I haven't time.
> I'd like to pray, but I haven't time.
> . . . .
> Lord, I have time,
> I have plenty of time,
> All the time that you gave me,
> The years of my life,
> The days of my years,
> The hours of my days,
> They are all mine
> Mine to fill, completely, up to the brim,
> To offer them to you, that of their insipid water
> You may make a rich wine such as you made once in
>   Cana of Galilee.
> I am not asking you tonight, Lord
>   for time to do this or then that,
> But your grace to do conscientiously, in the time
>   that you give me, what you want me to do.[18]

Leisure as the sphere of self-definition

In a predominately work-orientated society it is a man's job which gives him self-definition. This is where he proves himself; this is where he measures his self-potential and finds meaning in life. "The experience of having proven one's self, of having found a work, a sphere of consequential action, is precisely the experience through which we come to understand the meaning of human dignity."[19]

As the leisure society moves in upon us, work tends to lose its value for self-definition. Many people experience feelings of alienation in their work. Instead of work, leisure-time activities tend to become the sphere of self-realization. It is through hobbies, travel, community service, sailing, or skiing that persons find fulfillment. Self identities become established more by leisure activities than by work.

Dr. H. Clair Amstutz in a paper read to the Mennonite Recreation Study Conference in 1956 made the astute observation that Benjamin Franklin, for all his exhortations to work, retired at the age of 45 and gave himself over to avocational interests. Paradoxically, it is for these activities such as writing, scientific tinkering, and civic accomplishments that he is remembered rather than for his proficiency as a printer.[20]

Much has been said on the negative side about the boredom and emptiness of those who seek pleasure and happiness as an end in their recreation. They try so hard to be happy, compelling themselves to do things which they may not even like to do just because it is the accepted mode of fun, whether it be mountain climbing, going to parties, taking a vacation trip, or finding refuge in hobbies. In no instance are these forms of recreation to be criticized in themselves, but the compelling attitude with which they are engaged can be questioned. In such cases work, achievement, or personal advancement are masquerading as pleasure.[21]

On the positive side leisuretime activities may serve to meet particular inner needs which all of us possess. Here are several types of recreational activity:

1. Those which satisfy the acquisitive instinct. The urge to acquire or collect is met by one of the collecting hobbies — stamps, coins, salt and pepper shakers, books, etc.
2. Those which satisfy the creative urge, the desire to make something, to produce something useful or beautiful — woodworking, cooking, gardening, oil painting, the vast gamut of arts and crafts.
3. Those which work out one's drive for activity — games and other pursuits where one matches his skill or wit against a person or thing. Included here are such activities as tennis, basketball, ping-pong, competitive table games, hunting, and fishing.
4. Those which provide the opportunity for one to excel in the exercise of a skill — swimming or skating, piano playing, or vocal singing.
5. Those which satisfy the aesthetic appreciations, the love for the beautiful — reading poetry, visiting an art gallery, listening to good music, or viewing the beauties of nature.
6. Those which fulfill the needs for fellowship and association — visiting friends, parties, or other group social activities.
7. Those which provide the opportunity for service — tending the "Lord's acre," singing for the aged or ill, helping a neighbor.[22]

Leisure provides a creative function in life when it yields a new self-identity, a fresh God-consciousness, and an awakened social awareness. As suggested, the patterns by which this is accomplished are numerous and varied. Those leisure experiences which expose us to new sights and feelings, which bring us into contact with friends and comrades, which teach us varied skills and attitudes, and which restore our faith in God, all help us discover anew who we are. These are the experiences of self-definition which refresh and renew us.

Such an opportunity came into my experience during an interlude in the process of this writing project. In 1971 while on a travel-seminar to places of historic Anabaptist interest in Europe, our group had a free day in the Austrian Alps late in the month of June. After lunch that day I set out alone to hike on a post road hiking trail which led close by our guesthouse. The trail climbed up through the forest following alongside a swiftly flowing river whose chalky-white waters were coming from the melting snows in the upper elevations. After two hours of hiking, the trail brought me out above the tree line in the high Alpine meadows. Far ahead, or so it seemed, lay the glacier with the mountain pass still farther on. I set as my goal to reach the glacier, if possible.

Around me was a sight of incredible beauty: meadows lush with flowers, high rocky cliffs to the left and right, and every so often a waterfall spilling down across the rocks. The weather that afternoon was quite changeable. The sun was out sometimes; at other times it was hidden by clouds or by several brief snow squalls. In that high country I had the feeling of being virtually alone on God's great earth. (I met only several other hikers abroad that afternoon.)

Along the way I came to a miniature chapel right by the trail, obviously provided for travelers. I tried the door; it was open. The inside floor measurements of the chapel could not have exceeded six by eight feet. On each side of a narrow aisle were three single pews, making room for a capacity seating of six persons. In front was a miniature altar with artificial flowers. The only light came in through a small window on each side. I sat in the middle pew, right side, by the window to rest for a few minutes, and to pray — thanking God for bringing such marvelous providence and beauty into my life that day.

Refreshed, I moved on, eventually reaching the edge of the glacier, where it was possible to walk out on the snow. Retracing my steps that afternoon I arrived back at the guesthouse, the entire hike taking seven hours. To me, that afternoon was a leisure happening of self-definition, a celebration of wholeness in my life.

Frederick Nietzsche, the German philosopher, expressed eloquently this effect of nature upon the human soul as follows:

> The woods, the rocks, the winds, the vulture, the flowers, the butterfly, the meads, the mountain slopes, must all speak to him in their own language; in them, he must, as it were, come to know himself again in countless reflections and images, in a variegated round of changing visions; and in this way he will unconsciously

and gradually feel the metaphysical unity of all things in the great image of nature, and at the same time tranquilize his soul in the contemplation of her eternal endurance and necessity.[23]

Leisure as an expression of Christian vocation

Rural life in former years had a way of combining work and leisure. It was natural to mix the beauty of the sunset with the scent of new-mown hay, of teaching biology while caring for a newborn calf, of making a social event of corn-husking. It was easy to blend material production and spiritual experiences. The farmer planted and cultivated the crops and cared for the livestock, but it was God's providences of sun and rain which produced the increase. A bountiful harvest called forth a natural response of thanksgiving to God.

The spiritual significance of work has often been illustrated by the story of the man who asked three stonemasons what they were doing. The one was hewing stones, the second was earning a living for his family, the third was building a cathedral. The moral of the story, of course, was built on the response of the third man. Emil Brunner, however, said that he would preach on the second because in providing for his family the worker was doing a more important task religiously than building a cathedral.[24]

In our present industrial economy we are reminded of two realities which affect our theology of work and leisure. First, there is no longer a close relationship between a man's work and leisure. His working on the assembly line between the punches on the time clock is quite separated from his free time after 4:00 p.m.

and over the weekends. His work and leisure tend to be two different worlds, each with their own set of interests, skills, and values.

Second, there is little of religious significance in what many persons produce at their work. There is little to get excited about in producing part EX49G72. The inherent satisfaction in performing many jobs is of remote significance.

As noted before, a Christian's vocation is more than his job. A Christian lives his vocation not only through his work but also through his leisure. As Harvey Cox aptly stated:

> The call which comes to man from the Bible, the *vocatio*, summons him not to a job, but to joy and gratitude in whatever he is doing. It is equally relevant at work and at play — or in the "new leisure" in which work can be endowed with the quality of play.[25]

A Christian considers his leisure not as an end in itself, nor as the opposite of work, but as a function in his life which contributes to his calling. He views rest, relaxation, fun, and various kinds of leisure time activity in light of how they enhance or detract from this vocation.

One way in which Christians have exemplified their concern for vocation during their free time has been in their response to service opportunities. It is to the credit of Christian people that as they developed surplus resources in money and leisure time around the turn of the last century these resources were frequently used in missionary and service activities. Individuals spent their spare time over weekends going to the city or rural area to establish an outreach. Surplus personnel and finance were shared in a whole range of voluntary activities which served others and extended the church. True, such activity may have been approached with a sense of duty, but the time and energy involved represented nonwork rather than job time.

Leisure theorists today are promoting the same principle of shared public service as the best medicine for the new leisure class. Leo Perlis states:

> The untapped mental and emotional resources of the man who has no mental or emotional commitment to his job cry out for nourishment and are at the same time a potential source of mental and emotional commitment to his community and his fellow men, in short, a potential source for public service.[26]

"Purpose through public service" as a general leisure time slogan parallels closely the opportunity which God's people have in using their leisure in the furtherance of their calling in the world.

Harvey Cox in *The Secular City* enumerates the three basic functions of the servant church as *kerygmatic* (proclamation); *diakonic* (reconciliation, healing, service); and *koinoniac* (visible demonstration of the character of a new society).[27] The freedom of leisure provides a greater opportunity than ever before for Christians to carry out the tasks of the servant church. The new leisure provided by technological advances is truly part of God's providence which makes it possible for us today to express Christian vocation in ways which our forefathers did not have.

In Praise of Leisure

Leisure as a realm of responsible decision-making

Just as was noted for the concept of work, leisure, too, is a morally neutral concept. Leisure is neither good nor bad in itself. It must be judged in terms of stewardship principles, the motives involved, how our activities affect others, and how they influence our own lives. Judged on these bases, leisure has very definite value connotations.

In terms of character formation the manner in which free time is used is of importance. In one's regular work there are usually few consequential choices made day by day. Work hours and duties vary relatively little and demand few important moral choices. The same is true about the auxiliary time a person spends on the necessary duties of human existence such as sleeping, eating, dressing, and other daily functions. These routines are so well established, in fact, that they are largely habitual for all of us.

The use of leisure time, however, is another matter. Leisure time is the arena of choice. Here we must make decisions every day about how to use free time. We cannot evade leisure-time choices, even a non-choice amounts to a choice by default. If it is true that character is formed "at the forks of the road," this implies great moral consequence in the leisure choices we make.

The way in which a society uses its leisure time has been regarded by sociologists as an important factor in the formation of culture. The Neumeyers in their classic volume on *Leisure and Recreation* wrote this introductory statement:

> Society may find its greatest asset in the constructively used leisure of its citizens, but leisure may become also the greatest menace to our civilization. The civilizations of the world have been made and unmade by the way in which people have used their spare time. It matters not so much what people do when they work as what they do when they do not work.[28]

Leisure choices involve important decisions both as to types of activities and priorities of time. While specific leisure directives are few in the Bible there are a number of principles which are applicable. For instance, the Apostle Paul when instructing the young man, Timothy, writes "Train yourself in godliness. Exercise for the body is not useless, but godliness is useful in every respect, possessing, as it does, the promise of life now, and of the life which is soon coming."[29] Another word from Paul says: "What? know ye not that your body is the temple of the Holy Ghost which is in you, which ye have of God, and ye are not your own? For ye are bought with a price: therefore glorify God in your body, and in your spirit, which are God's."[30]

Leisure as an accrument of true wealth

As work involves an effort and a striving toward a result, leisure brings a kind of contentment, enjoyment, and freedom. These are the accruments of true wealth which are the very essence of leisure. Leisure in this sense is an ideal, the attainment of a state where it becomes possible to engage in activities for their own sake — to read, to hike, to garden, to sit in the sun for the enjoyment of it, to play tennis and to fish for the sake of playing and fishing, rather than for the sake of winning and catching.[31]

In an economy where the emphasis has been on the importance of work, it requires adjustment to the fact that modern technology offers to free us from the producer-materialist cycle. The revolutionary idea "that man shall not live by bread alone" is not easy to accept. One of the difficult adjustments, for instance, of old age is to recognize the change of role from lifelong producer to life as a consumer. It is hard to define usefulness except in terms of material goods. Dr. H. Clair Amstutz in speaking of an ideal for older persons says:

> If during his working lifetime he had caught the vision of the worth of personality, the value of the exchange of love and affection, of information for its own sake, of the beauties of nature, and had cultivated these pleasures, he would be very happy now in the enjoyment of people, truth, and beauty.[32]

Leisure offers the opportunity for a kind of disengagement from the work spiral. Even while we are engaged in our job responsibilities, our busy schedules, and complicated careers, leisure can provide us with a spirit that frees us from complete dependence upon work. A Christian understanding of leisure challenges us to an essentially spiritual concept which links our efforts in time with the eternal. It helps us look back on a day's work with a note of thanks irrespective of how much we get done or left undone. It bids us look forward to the excitement of a new day and the freshness and wonder of new experiences. It helps us define our roles in life and set up priorities as to what we can and should do. It prevents us from getting bogged down with excessive schedules, duties, and worries. It frees us to question the importance of both material and kingdom duties.

William Stevens, Jr., notes that genuine leisure is only possible for the man of faith in God. A man of idolatrous faith cannot know true leisure because he is possessed by his idols, be they work, gadgets, or even leisure pursuits. Conversely, faith in God frees man to enjoy and to participate. With his security in God, he is not bound by any activity, toy, or material thing. The accruments of true wealth are his in leisure. He is able to approach his leisure with the spirit of affirmation, celebration, and true freedom.[33]

Leisure as the soul of celebration

The fundamental justification for leisure according to Josef Pieper is celebration. He sees celebration as that point at which the three elements of leisure come to a focus: relaxation, effortlessness, and the superiority of "active leisure" to all functions. "If celebration is the core of leisure, then leisure can only be made possible and justifiable on the same basis as the celebration of a feast. That basis is divine worship."[34]

This theological basis for leisure is drawn from a very concrete idea in biblical history — the day of rest. To rest from work meant that time was reserved for divine worship. This definite period of time was set aside from the working days and hours and had no utilitarian ends. In fact, its object was quite in con-

In Praise of Leisure

trast to the rationale of work. It was a holy day, a feast day; its central activity was sacrifice, a voluntary offering freely given. Thus the act of worship created a store of real wealth which was unrelated to the workaday world.[35]

Ultimate leisure, therefore, is a divine time, a mental and spiritual attitude of inward calm and silence, a capacity for steeping oneself in the whole of creation, and climaxed in the act of celebration on holy days and feast days. Man must be more than worker if he is to lead a full human existence.[36]

In a recent book, *The Feast of Fools,* Harvey Cox speaks about two aspects of man's nature: *homo festivus* and *homo fantasia.*[37] Man not only works and thinks but he sings dances, prays, tells stories, and celebrates. He is a visionary dreamer and a mythmaker. These activities are at the very root of man's being. Cox calls for a renewal of our capacity and expression of festivity and fantasy. For centuries Christianity provided our civilization with the feast days that kept its history alive and with the images of the future that sustained its expectations. This needs to be revived through restoring the religious vitality of our holidays and celebrations. Our mechanized age dare not rob us of the capacity to imagine, to feel, and to celebrate. These functions lie at the very core of leisure.[38]

Leisure as internship for the eternal

Johann Huizinga entitled his study of the play element in culture, *Homo Ludens,* man the player. To call all human activity play is an old idea echoed variously by Plato ("men are the playthings of the gods"), by Shakespeare ("every man's an actor and all the world's a stage"), and by Luther (all creatures are God's masks and mummeries"). In the Book of Proverbs we find Wisdom saying, "The Lord possessed me in the beginning. . . . I was set up from eternity. . . . I was with him forming all things: and was delighted every day, playing before him at all times; playing in the world."[39]

To view all human activity as play from a divine standpoint is certainly not to depreciate such activity. Man's "playing" is serious, but it is not of ultimate seriousness. That is reserved for God. It is not our activity but God's activity that is of supreme importance. Our leisure is but an internship for our eternal life to come.

When Jesus visited in the home of Mary and Martha, he rebuked Martha who had served him but had complained about her sister merely listening to His teachings. Jesus said, "Martha, Martha, you are anxious and troubled about many things; one thing is needful. Mary has chosen the good portion, which shall not be taken away from her."[40]

The ultimate goal of man as described by the writer of Hebrews is rest. Man's temporal existence is a preparation, an internship for the eternal. In the present we are called to heed God's gracious invitation to believe and follow, so that in eternity we may receive the reward. A terse warning is expressed lest any of us come short of entering the promised rest. The faithful are assured of the promise. "There remaineth therefore a rest to the people of God. For he that is entered into his rest, he also hath ceased from

In Praise of Leisure 153

his own works, as God did from his. Let us labour therefore to enter into that rest."[41]

In praise of leisure

As Christians in every age seek to reinterpret God's truth for their particular setting, so we face the same challenge in the age of leisure. Today's leisure has evolved out of a rich historical-cultural background. The new leisure, recognized as a social change, promises to be of no less import than was the Industrial Revolution in its century of 1750-1850. This requires a reorientation of many of our habits and ways of thinking. It calls for a readjustment of our value structures. We face a social era quite different from what we have known in the past.

The church's frequent warnings in former years about leisure and leisure activities were not misplaced. Leisure has its hazards; the risk is acknowledged. Viewed from the vantage point of the traditional work ethic, the concerns about leisure were quite appropriate. They expressed in good conscience an application of Christian principles to the realities of that day.

Now it is our task to proceed just as diligently to assess the era of leisure and to apply the biblical principles which relate closely to the meanings and function of leisure. The fundamental concept of leisure is rich in content and value. A social ethic of leisure can be articulated that is compatible with the Christian faith.

And so we face the era of leisure as a fresh possibility to apply the Christian faith to life. We accept the unique possibilities and responsibilities which the leisure revolution forces upon us. We recognize the exciting new dimensions it can bring to our lives. We respond in praise of leisure because we accept it as a gift in the providence of God.

V. What the New Leisure Says to the Church

13. *The New Leisure—An Opportunity for the Church*

Wisdom cometh by opportunity of leisure. — *Unknown*

In a discerning analysis of the Christian in a leisure-oriented society Gordon J. Dahl points out the common confusion about work, play, and worship. "To put it sharply," he asserts, "most middle-class Americans tend to worship their work, to work at their play, and to play at their worship."[1] While this distortation of values has been with us for some time, it becomes even more apparent in the new leisure era. As Christians we are compelled to reconsider the priorities and relationships which work, play, and worship exert in our lives.

What is the Christian response to the new leisure? We need to examine this question not only as individuals but also within the context of the body of believers, the church. What specific challenges are brought to the church by the new leisure? How does leisure interrelate with the program of the church? What specific responses shall the local congregation make to the new leisure? What lifestyles will be appropriate to the Christian community within a leisure-oriented post-industrial society?

The call for a revised work-leisure ethic

A substitute principle for the sanctity of work is of first order. This does not imply a denial of the values of work but rather it means a new perspective for looking at work and leisure. The work ethic, for example, emphasized that leisure has to be earned, that the sole purpose of leisure is to re-create for more work, that leisure must be for the sake of something else, and that idleness is morally wrong. Happiness has been made a matter of material success and virtue a matter of usefulness. The utilitarian tendency has been so marked as to be fatal to the finer opportunities of leisure.

These values simply do not provide an adequate rationale for the leisure age. The attempt to hold on to work-oriented values in the new context forces people to several misconceptions. Either they experience a backwash of guilt and frustration about their abundance of free time or they swing to a fun morality simply to take up the time vacuum thrust upon them. What is needed is a revised social ethic to fit the era of advancing leisure.

The traditional work ethic structured human living into segments with time blocks allotted for work, schooling, transportation to and from the job, satisfying creature comforts, play, and recreation. Contrary to this

An Opportunity for the Church

frame of living, the new leisure ethic diminishes such time distinctions and focuses rather on a continuum concerned with man's quest for a higher quality of life.

Practically speaking, this ideal is not easy. Enjoyment, contentment, and freedom at leisure can be quite illusive. How else does one explain the vacation-blues syndrome, the Sunday "neurosis," and the depression that descends upon many people at Christmas and other holidays? Or the tendency to more tensions and interpersonal squabbles on a family vacation trip than when everyone is engaged in his usual activities at home?

The enjoyment of leisure cannot be taken for granted. A strong work and achievement orientation creates an imbalance of values which surfaces when we are not at work. We tend to fidget away our vacation and lose the benefits of relaxation.

Implementing a revised work-leisure ethic is a long-term project. Here are a few practical suggestions for vacation-type leisure. Vary your routine on vacations. Plan your activities for the next time off or vacation well ahead. Beware of the frantic vacation pace of trying to do too much, or travel too far, in too short a time. Come back from vacation a day early. Develop a sensible recreational pattern. Learn how to enjoy time off. Keep a conscious awareness of the contributing balance of work and leisure in your life.

In previous discussions we have laid a basis for belief and action about work and leisure from a contemporary Christian viewpoint. We receive leisure as a gift and not simply as a result of hard work. It comes as a kind of disengagement both from the production-consumption spiral and the frantic search for fun in our society. We legitimize leisure in our lives knowing that meaning and purpose develop not so much upon what we do as what we are. We recognize leisure's intrinsic worth and cultivate a capacity to enjoy leisure for what it contributes to the divine calling in our lives.

The need to resist pressures for leisure consumption

The fact of the economic boom in leisure-related products has already been noted. A few figures from a recent article in *U.S. News and World Report* underscore the mass force of leisure consumption in America. Spending for leisure in 1972 amounted to 105 billion dollars. About half of that was spent for recreational equipment and admission to sporting events, movies, concerts, and other cultural programs. Dollar sales of leisure equipment increased fifty-two percent in five years (1967-1972). In 1972 there were 72,000 motor homes produced, 200,000 travel trailers, and 228,000 tent trailers, plus several hundred thousand motorized recreational vehicles such as snowmobiles, minibikes, and dune buggies.[2]

Technological leisure dare not be allowed to destroy the very benefits which leisure is meant to have. In an article on "The Three-Day American Pleasure Trip" the writers cast this judgment:

> A man looking at a sublime mountain vista from the door of his multigadgeted camper may be where he is primarily for the sake of the camper and its gadgetry, not

An Opportunity for the Church 161

for the vista — and certainly not for the sublimity. . . . The motorized outdoorsman is drawn to the wilderness primarily to use the machinery, not to touch nature.[3]

Mobility, money, technology, and leisure are increasing intertwined in a seemingly endless spiral. Somewhere we need to resist the temptation to indulge in materialistic leisure and focus on leisure's intrinsic rewards and deep satisfactions. We must recognize that leisure gadgetry is only a means and not the end of leisure. How deeply to invest in leisure equipment is a major personal choice. The dangers of status-seeking and snobbishness in leisure activities and possessions are realities to be faced honestly. Brotherhood and stewardship principles must guide us in how we occupy free time and use resources for leisure.

> There is indeed a prophetic ministry to be taken up in a society that allows two million families to have second homes when there are still several million other families who are homeless. There is a message from God to be delivered to a people which spends more on its household pets than it does on its dependent senior citizens. There is a word from the Lord for a nation that spends more to kill each Vietnamese than to educate each American, a government that is more willing to guarantee fair profits for some of its powerful corporations than full stomachs for some of its powerless people.[4]

A concern for the natural environment

The centennial anniversary (1972) of the National Park Service brought considerable publicity to the problem of "urban blight" in some national recreational areas of the United States and the accompanying environmental destruction. Hordes of visitors leave their mark on national park and play areas. In Yellowstone National Park some of the small geysers have been choked with litter until they no longer erupt. In once beautiful campgrounds there are wide areas where even the green grass is gone. The overcrowding is due not so much to people as to the things which they bring along with them. Selected park areas have already moved to ban all private cars in certain places, substituting open-air minibuses where transportation is necessary.

The quality of leisure experiences in the outdoors is bound to the environment in which we live. Conservationists are determined to preserve the wilderness country where the balance of nature still exists and where the nature lover can truly enjoy God's earth. The preservation of natural areas will be of increasing importance as leisure time and leisure equipment for "roughing it" expand. The demand for conservation is of high priority. We need the kind of spiritual reverence for our natural environment as was expressed a century ago by the early naturalist, John Muir, who declared, "Mountain parks and reservations are useful not only as fountains of timber and irrigating rivers but as fountains of life. Everyone needs beauty as well as bread, places to play in and pray in, where nature may heal and cheer and give strength to body and soul alike."[5]

The flexibility of leisure-time patterns

With the four-day workweek already beginning to surface we face increased variations of work and leisure-time patterns. Technologically, it is possible for a worker to fulfill his obligation by working half a month, half a year, or half a working lifetime. Vastly increased options on how one proportions his work and leisure are already evident. The 13-week sabbatical every five years won recently by the United Steelworkers is an omen of the future. Leisure taken in block time is not the same as having an equal number of free days scattered singly over a five-year span. Differing combinations of work, schooling, and vacation periods will alter lifestyles in America and force leisure-time options radically different from the past.

The possibilities of earlier retirement

Increased pension plans and benefits influence workers to enter retirement at an earlier age. If working half a lifetime is already a technological possibility a person could retire at forty or before, having put behind him a full quota of productive work. He could then look forward to thirty or forty years of retirement beginning in the very "prime of life."

If, however, his sense of worth has been attached to his job, what meaning can such a retiree derive from his extended years at leisure? Can feelings of uselessness and rejection in the retirement years be replaced by the assurance that the retiree is wanted, needed, and belongs, and that his life still contributes. Actually his earlier retirement, better physical health, and longer life-span all offer distinct opportunities for a useful senior life.

The influence of the counterculture in leisure

The influence of the counterculture presents a challenge of contemporary note. Casting suspicion on middle-class America's consumption patterns, many youth are questioning the necessity of possessing a conglomeration of leisure gadgets for the mere sake of owning them. As pointed out in a recent article by James F. Murphy the counterculture is essentially a new leisure class. Rejecting external standards of leisure attainment, the payoff comes from simply letting leisure happen and enjoying its inherent benefits. The leisure of the counterculture is characterized by various rituals, chivalry, celebrations, community sharing, freer time reference, and intrinsic fulfillment. There is an integration of the affective and intellectual experiences and a rejection of often boring and narrowing influences of the technocratic society.[6]

Gordon J. Dahl identifies five aspects in the emerging leisure ethic:

> It is based upon a radical affirmation of personal freedom, based upon the inherent dignity and uniqueness of every human being. It presupposes a pluralistic system of values and promotes a wide diversity of life styles. It compels the integrity, but dispels the permanence, of human relationships and replaces narrow group loyalties with more ecumenical attitudes and interests. It prefers immediate satisfaction over promises of future happiness. And it advances the interdependence of men and groups instead of their independence and competition.[7]

It is interesting to note how closely these five points parallel the values expressed by those who have been angered and alienated by established systems

An Opportunity for the Church

in American society. His first point is the "do your own thing" philosophy, which Dahl sees as a contemporary counterpart to the Protestant doctrine of calling. This is an affirmation of freedom, uniqueness, and personal dignity in the face of society's dehumanizing forces. One may do his "thing" in leisure; he may do it in work. But in any case in the Christian context it springs from the freedom which we have through commitment to Christ.[8]

In second place, and a corollary of the first idea, is the acceptance of alternate lifestyles and value systems. Everyone is not cut out over the same pattern; more diversity will exist. This becomes a challenge to the Christian for the development of more authentic and creative ways of living. The third aspect of the new leisure ethic is a recognition that human relationships will become more meaningful but less permanent. Attachments to a particular job or locality or circle of friends will give way to more mobility and wider concepts of belonging. Obviously this has its hazards, but also makes for more opportunities of involving oneself as a Christian.[9]

The fourth aspect has to do with the urge to "live now," in opposition to the principle of deferred rewards. The mass media constantly bombard us with this kind of philosophy. Dahl comments, "If Christianity is to vie for loyalties in the leisure oriented society, it will have to offer peace and joy in the here and now as well as an ultimate hope."[10] Finally, leisure values are forcing us to more interdependence. We have to learn to work, play, and re-create with each other. The age of strict individualism is over. In

Christian terms, we are called increasingly to a lifestyle of sharing.[11]

While youth and the counterculture have helped to shape the new leisure there are many people young and older who are accepting the new leisure styles. Many Americans are looking to the freedom of leisure for new values and meanings. The church dare not ignore these challenges in the leisure age.

Leisure and the program of the church

The mission of the church is to be the body of Christ. Called out from the world the church brings into existence a new society, the people of God. The Apostle Peter speaks of this Christian community as "a royal priesthood, an holy nation, a peculiar [separated] people."[12] The church provides a fellowship for its members and sets up an environment conducive to the practice of Christian virtues.

The church is the custodian of truth and acts as the salt of the earth and the light of the world. It is concerned about the nurture of its members "until Christ be formed in you."[13] It provides opportunities for corporate worship and demonstrates the love of God in a visible way within the brotherhood.

Finally, the church seeks for the restoration, redemption, and renewal of all people. It is commissioned to go into all the world proclaiming and witnessing the glad tidings of salvation. It speaks in a prophetic role against the evils of society and serves in loving responsibility to meet human needs.

Relating leisure and the program of the church it is immediately evident that the church carries out many of its functions in leisure time. While the church is concerned primarily with the ultimate issues of life (salvation, faith, meaning of existence, human destiny) its program provides activities which yield leisure-time benefits in a secondary way. Obviously, what the Christian does in leisure should be consistent and not detract from the mission of the church. The new leisure offers ever greater opportunities for Christians to carry out the tasks of the servant church. Additional time and resources for leisure add to our responsibility to exercise the divine calling in a new context.

To minister effectively to people in a leisure society the church takes leadership first in defining its own role in the world. While the church legitimately engages in the secondary role of providing leisure, as we shall note later, it keeps central its primary mission as Christ's body in the world. If the church were to consider itself only in a self-serving function with respect to leisure, it could simply provide more programs and facilities for its already leisure-burdened members. Some groups have approached their leisure responsibility in this fashion. Rudolph Norden warns in his book, *The Church Encounters the New Leisure,* "When the Church follows this tack it becomes a glorified tension-relieving, hand-holding, baby sitting agency in behalf of itself."[14]

Church-sponsored leisure studies

Since the church today exists in a culture shifting from a work orientation to a leisure orientation, another of its tasks is to come to a better understanding of the new leisure, its influences and moral implications. The church wrestles with the ethics of leisure decision-making and helps its people in mastering their leisure opportunities. In a formal way the church performs this function through studies which look at the facts of leisure, articulate principles, suggest programs, and offer guidelines for action. In this connection several denominational studies on leisure are worth noting.

In 1961 the National Council of Churches initiated studies on leisure which culminated in two mimeographed reports and a major book by Robert Lee, director of the study. The NCC has since convened regional conferences and established a Task Force on Leisure. It offers assistance to denominations and to state and local councils of churches in initiating and developing leisure ministries at resorts and state parks.

On several occasions the Jewish Theological Seminary of America has sponsored conferences on leisure, producing a round of serious studies on the subject. Roman Catholics and numerous Protestant groups such as the United Church of Christ and the Southern Baptist Convention have commissions working on the problems of leisure and on establishing various kinds of leisure ministries. Campus Crusade and Inter-Varsity Christian Fellowship have been active in witnessing to college students on the beaches.

The Mennonite Church entered seriously into the study of leisure through the work of a Recreation Study Committee appointed in 1954 by the Mennonite Commission for Christian Education. A study conference in 1956 brought together the thought and experience of the church on the subject. This work culminated with a Position Statement on Recreation adopted by the Mennonite General Conference in session at Johnstown, Pennsylvania, on August 25, 1961.[15] Subsequently, several of the district conferences conducted similar study sessions on the implications of recreation and leisure to the program of the church.

Leisure-time guidance

The church has the task of helping orient people to the new leisure and its possibilities. Many people are fearful of leisure partly because they feel guilty when they are not working and also because they are unsure about what to do in their free time. Leisure may be forcing persons to think about how empty and futile their lives really are apart from work. They are afraid to meditate, to ponder, to ask questions, or to learn new skills. Their whole life has been bound up in their work and when the job is threatened or gone they are up against a sudden emptiness.

The church helps people to think about their values in life and assists individuals in making adjustments to changing work-leisure patterns. One of the big tasks is simply to legitimize leisure, to prepare Christians for living creatively in a changing culture. An appreciation of the work-leisure rhythm is a beginning point. The church assists persons to see life as a whole, not as competing parts.

There are specific opportunities for the church to offer its members guidance for leisure-time activities. All ages within the church need practical suggestions geared to meet their needs. Youth with the abundance of free time need activity outlets. Busy parents who are deeply involved in starting their families and vocational careers need another type of guidance, while middle-aged people with successful active lives need other assistance. Perhaps the greatest opportunity is with those approaching or already in retirement. After a busy and rewarding life of work they need help in adjusting to a change of pace. In addition to these general needs there are individuals who have particular problems of adjustment in which the church can help, such as those with enforced leisure due to unemployment, under-employment, illness or disability, or those with a changed job or profession.

The matter of leisure consumption is another concern of the church. Christian stewardship principles need to be presented so that families and groups can make decisions involving how to spend their resources in leisure and what leisure equipment they should acquire. The matter of leisure and vacation planning and expenditures might be made an item for the receiving and giving of counsel within the brotherhood.

The church helps Christians formulate principles for occupying a part of their leisure time for their own use. Persons need to see constructive creative possibilities rather than merely time-consuming spectator types of nonactivity. The importance of choice in leisure and the principles for its use should be taught. Some need to learn the lessons of relaxation and letting-go; others may need help toward more constructive activities. The meaning of leisure must be emphasized so that persons can develop an operational philosophy consistent with Christian principles.

The spiritual potential of leisure time must be emphasized — how God speaks to us through the beauties of nature, through the experiences of human relationship, through meditation, reflection and prayer, and through the personal study of the Scriptures. Through many of the free-time experiences of life we are reminded of God's order and care, His providence and love. Leisure gives us the time to wonder and to search. To look at the stars on a clear night, to watch the changing panorama of a sunset reflected in the clouds, to listen to the waves of the ocean, to engage true friends in deep conversation — these are the moments of leisure.

In helping individuals build a personal philosophy of leisure, the church speaks from the standpoint of the Christian calling. When persons have a clear commitment to Christian vocation, then the relationships of work and leisure are better understood. Both need to contribute ultimately to the faith pilgrimage in Christ.

As suggested earlier, a distinction between job and work may be helpful particularly in cases where one's job may be less than meaningful. At times a person may accept or be forced on a temporary basis to a job which is simply a way of earning a livelihood and little more. It may be possible for one's leisure to make direct contributions to his work so that a real sense of meaning ties together all that one does under the lordship of Christ.

The church also has a responsibility to exercise the function of judgment in leisure. Through establishing guidelines and principles, leisure activities may be evaluated and defensible decisions made. The church warns against activities which are morally wrong and have an atmosphere which is ungodly and corrosive to spiritual and physical life. It points out other activities which may be amoral in themselves and must be judged on such bases as their associations, their influence, and the degree to which they may conflict with the church's program. It encourages those activities which are good and yield true leisure values. The meaningful, constructive use of leisure is a concern of the church.

Christian service as a leisure opportunity

The church provides many activities within its program which occupy leisure time with positive benefits. This occurs in worship services, study classes, fellowship groups, service activities, recreational programs, retreats, and renewal experiences. Summer camping programs sponsored by the church have in some cases developed into year-round programs with emphasis on church renewal. The church through its Christian education agencies supplies leisure time and recreational program ideas for use in the congregation. Church-sponsored leisure activities often include the element of service. A very important leisure benefit is found in the satisfaction of doing something for somebody else.

Much Christian service is done in leisure time, commonly called "marginal time." With less time required for work and for the related maintenance tasks of life, a wider margin of time is open for voluntary activity in the church. Many individuals regularly give

An Opportunity for the Church

time to disaster service, to long- or short-term service projects, to community service, to evangelism and witness, to visiting the sick, to counseling and sharing time with a friend or neighbor.

God's people have a good record of sharing their leisure time in projects for the benefit of others. The church needs to foster this. Every community needs the voluntary services of persons to carry on projects in the interest of the community. Many public service organizations depend almost entirely upon people giving part of their leisure time. Parents are called upon to participate in P.T.A., to serve as committee members for the Red Cross, or to help with the Little League program.

No doubt the most significant opportunities for leisure and retirement-time service are made available through the service and mission agencies of the church. There are many things to be done by the church. The challenge is to match person and task.

14. The New Leisure—Implications for the Congregation

> But yield who will to their separation
> My object in living is to unite
> My avocation and my vocation
> As my two eyes are one in sight.
> Only when love and need are one
> And the work is play for mortal stakes
> Is the deed ever truly done
> For heaven and the future's sake.
> — Robert Frost

In bringing things together in this final chapter the focus will be placed on the congregation because it is here that Christians meet and interact as they carry out Christ's mandate in the midst of the world. The congregation gathers to worship and instruct; it scatters to witness and serve. In a tangible way it forms the body of Christ at the local level. Within the congregation Christians act and interact on life issues such as work and leisure. What each member does has a corporate effect upon the group of believers. Here is where the patterns of the new leisure will be lived in Christian community.

Adjusting the congregational program

Three-day weekends, longer vacations, and increased mobility already threaten traditional patterns of congregational life. With Sunday fading into the weekend it becomes more difficult for the congregation to gather for its worship services. Church members who in the past were usually at home on Sundays may now be on the road. The attendance at the Sunday morning worship services especially over holidays and during the summer months becomes quite irregular, with Sunday evening attendance even more sporadic. The customary patterns of worship in the congregation have plenty of competiton. Many congregations regularly experience an exodus of their members on Sundays to the church camp, lake retreat, or winter resort.

Dutch theologian J. C. Hoekendijk suggests that the congregation might adjust its calendar to the schedule of society. He sees precedence for this in the past.

> Perhaps instead of the fifty-two Sundays, we should have ten or fifteen "Christ days" per year, festive occasions, and in between gatherings at times when people are really there? When we adamantly hold on to our ecclesiastical calendar, we easily might turn it into a religious calendar, according to which it is imposed upon people to make time for God. I thought that in the church we would want to follow an evangelical calendar through which it becomes apparent that God has time for man. What are the implications in this connection of the saying that "man has

not been created for the Sabbath, but the Sabbath has been created for man"?[1]

When Sunday was the only nonwork day the activities of the congregation could be centered at that time. In the future we may need to plan other satisfactory meeting times for the congregation. While Sunday will no doubt remain the important time for worship services because of tradition and because of the meaning of the day, the congregation might provide a major worship service on a week night to accommodate those persons not present over the weekend. The hours of the regular services on Sunday might be shifted one way or the other for the convenience of people during the various seasons of the year.

New forms of congregational activity

Congregations are already experimenting with new forms to meet the needs of various groups within the church. On occasions a congregation may move its Sunday services to a nearby camp or retreat area. Breakfast meetings for business and professional persons, luncheon meetings for people downtown, religious education classes for children after the school days, or an occasional all-night vigil for the youth are other schedule adaptations to accommodate particular groups.

The congregation ought to serve people where they are. If on weekends people congregate at camping sites and lakesides, these are the places where a worship service can be held. In the outdoors and with a simple format an effective ministry can be provided for this transient group. Some congregations actively invite guests staying at local motels to attend their services

Implications for the Congregation

and may even share the hospitality of their homes for Sunday dinner with the tourists. Each congregation should assess its particular possibilities for leisure ministry and try to meet those needs.

The congregation should provide opportunities for sharing among members on how they live out their Christian vocation through their work and leisure. This, of course, needs to be broader than the usual kinds of reporting we have considered in the past from full-time Christian workers or missionaries. What experiences of spiritual significance has the Christian automobile salesman had? What contacts did a Christian family make at the campgrounds where they were vacationing? What community needs does the Christian social worker have to share?

We need to hear from each other in our work and leisure. We need to affirm each other in the Christian calling at the places where we work and recreate. We need to commission individuals for spiritual witness in their particular work or leisure situation. We need to assist others with the burdens and concerns of everyday life. If in the congregation we could get this total view of vocation, work, and leisure we could have a more effective impact as God's people than we ever did with a more fragmented approach which separated leisure, work, and Christian calling.

Arnold Cressman says that "Christian education must help persons in the local congregation to see their lives whole, not with a good and bad part, not with a full and empty part, but as a whole life all of which has purpose and meaning in the eyes of God."[2] In this way we can begin to relate to other people as Jesus did, to hear, to understand, and to help our neighbors. This is the example of Jesus, who had time to relate deeply to the needs of the Samaritan woman at the well.

The congregation has the challenge to capitalize upon the nonwork time of its members in fulfilling its local mission. There are the usual service opportunities — teaching in the Sunday school, ushering, singing with the choir, and serving on committees. A poll might be conducted to find out what talents or interests members have concerning congregational tasks and leisure activities. The idea is not to stifle personal leisure but to assemble data useful to the church in its program. Opportunities for service, fellowship, and witness can easily develop from such a start. Persons of similar interests recreationally can get together. Leisure problems can become leisure opportunities if people can be matched with meaningful activities.

By identifying gifts which can be cultivated and used the congregation is helping people view themselves in a holistic way. Human gifts can often be exercised both in work and leisure situations. The person with secretarial skills can apply these not only in the office on the job but also on the church council on a leisure-time basis. Whether one's gifts at work and at leisure complement each other or are of an unrelated kind, they may be utilized in the congregational program. Lack of recognition of human resources has been a serious charge against the church in the past. Viewed in the context of Christian vocation God's gifts through persons will be used much more fully than when we tended to pigeonhole people and activities in the church.

If the congregation has a purposeful program, members in their nonwork time can be involved in mission closer home instead of only supporting programs which send people to distant parts of the world. The carpenter-builder may take time off to assist in disaster operations. The teacher may have full summers available for helping in church camps. A businessman may take several days per week or weeks per year to assist at a church institution on a minimal support or gratis basis. Individuals who have successful careers and are now at an age where their children have been raised and educated might turn partially or fully to the service of the church in their community even before retirement age.

The congregation should help individuals identify various options of activity into which they might go as more free time opens up for them. Such a program seriously implemented in the congregation would alter lifestyles, as well as help fulfill the mission of the church. From an emphasis on "accumulate till I come" we might obey more fully Christ's imperative to "occupy till I come." The "voluntary service" philosophy which heretofore has been associated primarily with youth and with service in a distant place needs to be thought of more broadly. Leisure has opened up opportunities for more of us to share in the direct mission of the congregation in our communities on a self-supporting basis. Creative congregations will take the initiative. The possibilities for involvement cannot even be anticipated fully at present.

A word of caution should be offered that the congregation does not try to fill up everyone's free time with an assortment of activities, even of a churchly type. To provide a flood of activities merely to occupy people's time is not the answer. Hopefully the congregation can respect and encourage in its members the basic freedom which leisure implies. Stevens puts the primary responsibility of the congregation into perspective by asserting, "The task of the church is not so much to monopolize a man's time with a wealth of activities as to monopolize his spirit, to make it one with Jesus Christ."[3]

The congregation ministers to leisure-time needs

A particular group to which the congregation should minister are those who have leisure time forced upon them. They may be idle but not by their own choice. Consequently they may find leisure more a burden than a joy. The unemployed or semi-employed, seasonal and migratory workers, the physically handicapped, and those who are ill have all been reduced partially or totally to involuntary leisure. The congregation should meet these needs and help individuals convert pointless time to purposeful time.

A related leisure concern by the congregation is to face realistically what happens to individuals when their work time is reduced either by retirement or by a curtailment of jobs in the leisure age. Christian education has the task of reorienting thinking about work. In the past people worked long and hard to be good servants and stewards. In the future the ethical thing may well be to limit work to the level of making

Implications for the Congregation

a living so that jobs can be shared with others.

A program of graduated retirement whereby the working hours are phased out gradually rather than the current practice of an abrupt halt would help to ease the adjustment of retirement as well as open up more time for service opportunities. Another possibility would be a wider use of the sabbatical year, or some other form of leisure-interspersed periods of time. Both employers and employees might take off occasionally for a time of study, relaxation, or working in a different setting. This would be a way of extending their service, as well as refreshing themselves.

Meaningful religious celebrations

Perhaps the most important response to the new leisure which the congregation can provide through its own program is to energize the memory and hope of our Christian faith. As God's people we have a great heritage. We are part of a larger story; we are in the continuing of God's action with men. We have a history; we have a future.

The congregation provides the experiences of worship and study, song and ritual which give meaning to the past action of God and extend the frontiers of hope into the future. It is in the fellowship of the congregation that we learn to recognize the origins and destiny of our faith. Through the important events of the Christian calendar we are supplied with the memories and aspirations so vital to our lives.

Harvey Cox speaks of the price which affluent industrialized Western man has paid while "gaining the whole world and losing its soul."

Today something seems to be wrong. Our feast days have lost their vitality. Christmas is now largely a family reunion, Easter a spring style show, and on Thanksgiving there is no one to thank. The potency has drained from the religious symbols that once kept us in touch with our forebears. The images that fired our hopes for the future have lost their glow. We often see the past as a cage from which we must escape, and the future as a dull elongation of what we now have.[4]

The best response to this indictment lies within the powers of the Christian church. The congregation needs to put real meaning into its religious holidays and celebrations. It needs to encourage the celebrative and imaginative faculties within its group. It must provide the opportunities for song, ritual, and vision which link us to the Christian faith. Through the leadership of the congregation we need to renew our capacity for festivity and fantasy. In the new leisure age this becomes all the more important as technological advances tent to impoverish not only our work but also our leisure.

Leisure and worship

Josef Pieper struggled with the philosophical questions of "what makes leisure inwardly possible and, at the same time, what is its fundamental justification?"[5] The answer to both these questions is worship, Pieper declares. Both the possibility of leisure and its ultimate justification have roots in divine worship. The day of rest meant time reserved for worship. A particular place, the temple, was especially reserved and marked off from the rest of the land which was used for agri-

Implications for the Congregation

culture and habitation. At this place and at stated times God's people celebrated in worship.

At the heart of worship was the act of sacrifice, a voluntary offering freely given. The offering of the best of the herd or the giving up of the firstfruits are acts completely antithetical to the principles of work and labor. Here in an act of wastefulness and deliberate squandering arises the essence of true wealth and gracious generosity. "The celebration of divine worship, then, is the deepest of the springs by which leisure is fed and continues to be vital."[6]

Although few may choose to equate leisure and worship as does Josef Pieper, many have noted the common denominators between worship and religion on the one hand and leisure and recreation on the other. One of the best summarizations of their common elements is found in Professor Charles K. Brightbill's *Man and Leisure.* He notes that both recreation and religion, to use his terms, are engaged in voluntarily. Each provides opportunities for renewal and for achieving balance and perspective in life. In both there is an opportunity to express inner desires. Individual choice and free will are characteristic of each. Both can provide man with dimension and grace.[7]

We do indeed recognize the distinct functions which worship and leisure fulfill in the life of the Christian. Leisure at its best contributes to worship. "Be still, and know that I am God."[8] The call is to come apart from an anxious and troubled life so that we can contemplate and commune with God. Leisure becomes a means to the experience of worship. John Preston Dever notes:

If man has no leisure, he cannot wonder; if he cannot wonder, then he cannot have the desire to fathom his spirit and the mystery of life and thus his religion grows cold. There is little joy in life. There is little hope. The rhythm of leisure-work brings one closest to the true celebration of life.[9]

Looking from the other side, worship and an honest relationship with God contribute to leisure at its best. A recognition of what God provides in His gifts of time, intelligence, the physical world, redemption, the capacity to give and receive love, all contribute to the abundant life. Christians know the joy and release which makes possible the transcendence of all of life — work and leisure.

To use a metaphor from the history of God's people, we are called to come up out of a land of toil and hard taskmasters to a land flowing with milk and honey. Perhaps at no time in history is such a promise so likely to be fulfilled, at least in its earthy sense, as in the era of the new leisure.

NOTES

CHAPTER 1

1. John Saar, "Family Plight: $14,365 a Year and No Fun," *The Washington Post* (March 11, 1973), pp. Al and A8.
2. *This Week Magazine, The Washington Sunday Star* (May 14, 1967), citing James A. Garfield, p. 1.
3. C. Wright Mills, *White Collar, the American Middle Classes* (New York: The Oxford University Press, 1951), p. 236.
4. *Ibid.*, p. 237.
5. Max Kaplan, "A New Language for a New Leisure," paper prepared for Regional Seminar on Interdisciplinary Studies, Association of Departments of English, Tampa, Florida (February 11, 1972), p. 11.
6. Staffan B. Linder, *The Harried Leisure Class* (New York: Columbia University Press, 1970), 182 pp.
7. *Ibid.*, pp. 94, 95.
8. *Ibid.*, pp. 47-53.

CHAPTER 2

1. Max Kaplan, "The Relevancy of Leisure," *Technology, Human Values and Leisure*, edited by Max Kaplan and Philip Bosserman (Nashville: Abingdon Press, 1971), p. 22.
2. *World Book Dictionary* (Chicago: Field Enterprises Educational Corporation, 1969), p. 1187.
3. Sebastian De Grazia, *Of Time, Work, and Leisure* (New York: Doubleday and Company, 1962), p. 332.
4. Walter Kerr, *The Decline of Pleasure* (New York: Simon & Schuster, 1965), p. 39.
5. Robert Lee, *Religion and Leisure in America* (New York: Abingdon

Press, 1964), p. 35.
6. Josef Pieper, *Leisure, the Basis of Culture* (New York: Pantheon Books, 1964), pp. 27-32.
7. Joffre Dumazedier, "Leisure," *International Encylopedia of the Social Sciences,* IX (New York;: Macmillan, 1968), pp. 250, 251.
8. Max Kaplan, "New Concepts of Leisure Today," The Lindeman Memorial Lecture, National Conference on Social Welfare, Dallas, Texas (May 17, 1971), p. 5.
9. Mark Twain, *The Adventures of Tom Sawyer* (New York: Harper, 1903), p. 30.
10. Johann Huizinga, *Homo Ludens, A Study of the Play Element in Culture* (Boston: Beacon Press, 1950), p. 13.
11. Robert Lee, *op. cit.,* pp. 76-89.
12. Richard C. Cabot, *What Men Live By* (New York: Houghton Mifflin Company, 1914), 341 pp.
13. Emmanuel G. Mesthene, "Technology and Humanistic Values," *Technology, Human Values, and Leisure,* edited by Max Kaplan and Philip Bosserman (Nashville, Abingdon Press, 1971), p. 42.
14. Ecclesiastes 3:1-3.
15. Robert Lee, "Leisure and Religion in American Culture," *Theology Today,* Vol. XIX, No. 1 (April 1962), p. 51.
16. Mark 1:15a.
17. Sebastian De Grazia, *op. cit.,* p. 86.

CHAPTER 3

1. Jay B. Nash, *Philosophy of Recreation and Leisure* (St. Louis: The C. V. Mosby Company, 1953), p. 13.
2. *Ibid.,* p. 89.
3. *Ibid.,* pp. 93-96.

CHAPTER 4

1. Jay B. Nash, *Recreation: Pertinent Readings* (Dubuque, Iowa: Wm. C. Brown Company, 1965), citing Robert Hutchins, p. 245.
2. Godby, Geoffrey, "Leisure: Nearing the Receding Horizon," *Parks and Recreation,* VI (August 1971), p. 33.
3. Juanita M. Kreps, *Lifetime Allocation of Work and Leisure,* Research Report No. 22 (Washington, D.C.: U.S. Department of Health, Education, and Welfare, 1968), p. 25.
4. *Ibid.,* p. 37.
5. Rudolph Norden, *The Christian Encounters the New Leisure* (St. Louis: Concordia, 1965), p. 16.
6. Max Kaplan, *Leisure in America: A Social Inquiry* (New York: Wiley and Sons, 1960), p. 294.
7. Herman Kahn and Anthony J. Wiener, *The Year 2000* (New York: Macmillan Company, 1967), p. 197.
8. Juanita M. Kreps, *op. cit.* p. 21.

Notes

9. *Ibid.*, p. 21.
10. Herman Kahn and Anthony J. Wiener, *op. cit.*, pp. 194-198.
11. Juanita K. Kreps, *op. cit.*, p. 16.
12. William Chapman, "The Early Retirement Ethic," *The Washington Post* (March 25, 1973), pp. A1 and A20.
13. Max Kaplan, *op. cit.*, p. 295.
14. Bertrand Russell, "In Praise of Idleness," *Mass Leisure*, edited by Eric Larrabee and Rolf Meyersohn (Glencoe, Illinois: The Free Press, 1958), pp. 99, 100.

CHAPTER 5

1. Richard Kraus, "Economics of Leisure Today," *Parks and Recreation*, VI (August 1971), p. 62.
2. "Investing in Companies That Profit for Pleasure," *Changing Times*, Vol. 25, No. 6 (June 1971), pp. 35-40.
3. Charles K. Brightbill, *The Challenge of Leisure* (Englewood Cliffs, New Jersey: Prentice-Hall, 1963), p. 33.
4. Eric Fromm, "Alienation Under Capitalism," *Man Alone*, edited by Eric and Mary Josephson (New York: Dell Publishing Company, 1962), pp. 56-73.
5. Clement Greenberg, "Work and Leisure under Industrialism," *Mass Leisure*, edited by Eric Larrabee and Rolf Meyersohn (Glencoe, Illinois: The Free Press, 1958), p. 40.
6. August Heckscher and Sebastian De Grazia, "Problems of Executive Leisure," *Harvard Business Review*, XXXVII (July-August, 1959), pp. 7-16.
7. Sebastian De Grazia, *Of Time, Work, and Leisure* (New York: Doubleday and Company, 1962), p. 64.
8. Robert Lee, *Religion and Leisure in America* (New York: Abingdon Press, 1964), pp. 40, 41.
9. Nels Anderson, *Work and Leisure* (New York: The Free Press of Glencoe, 1961), citing Joffre Dumazedier, p. 104.
10. Juanita M. Kreps, *op. cit.*, p. 16.
11. Gilbert Burck, "There'll Be Less Leisure Than You Think," *Fortune*, Vol. 81 (March 1970), p. 86.
12. Sebastian De Grazia, *op. cit.*, p. 67.
13. A. L. New, "Leisure Equals Opportunity . . . If," *International Journal of Religious Education*, Vol. 42 (May 1966), pp. 22, 23.
14. Charles A. Reich, *The Greening of America* (New York: Random House, 1970), pp. 194, 195.
15. Arthur Schlesinger, Jr., "Implications of Leisure," *Technology, Human Values, and Leisure*, edited by Max Kaplan and Philip Bosserman (Nashville: Abingdon Press, 1971), citing Max Frisch, p. 77.
16. Dero A. Saunders and Sanford S. Parker, "$30 Billion for Fun," *Fortune*, Vol. 49 (June 1954), p. 118.

CHAPTER 6

1. Charles A. Reich, *The Greening of America* (New York: Random

House, 1970), p. 181.
2. Arthur Schlesinger, Jr., "Implications of Leisure," *Technology, Human Values and Leisure*, edited by Max Kaplan and Philip Bosserman (Nashville: Abingdon Press, 1971), p. 77.
3. *Ibid.*, p. 77.
4. Ernest Havemann, "The Emptiness of Too Much Leisure," LIFE, LVI (February 14, 1964), p. 84.
5. Ernest Havemann, "The Task Ahead: How to Take Life Easy." *LIFE*, LVI (February 21, 1964), p. 88.
6. Bertrand Russell, "In Praise of Idleness," *Mass Leisure*, edited by Eric Larrabee and Rolf Meyersohn (Glencoe, Illinois: The Free Press, 1958), p. 99.
7. Robert MacIver, "The Great Emptiness," *Man Alone*, edited by Eric and Mary Josephson (New York: Dell Publishing Company, 1962), pp. 145-147.
8. Charles A. Reich, *op. cit.*, p. 195.

CHAPTER 7

1. Wayne E. Oates, *Confessions of a Workaholic* (New York: World Book Company, 1971), 112 pp.
2. *Ibid.*, p. 10.
3. Peter T. Chew, "Workaholics Fidget Away Vacations," *The National Observer* (June 30, 1973), quoting Francis L. Clark, p. 8.
4. Editorial in *LIFE*, Vol. 71, No. 10 (September 3, 1971), p. 8.
5. Sebastian De Grazia, *Of Time, Work, and Leisure* (Garden City, New York: Anchor Books, 1964), p. 211.
6. Mortimer J. Adler, "In Defense of the Philosophy of Education," Chapter V in *Philosophies of Education*, Forty-first Yearbook of the National Society for the Study of Education, ed. N.B. Henry, Part I (Chicago: the Society, 1942), p. 211.
7. *New York Times Magazine* (April 6, 1969), p. 54.
8. Robert S. Cohen, "On the Marxist Philosophy of Education," *Modern Philosophies and Education* Fifty-fourth Yearbook of the National Society for the Study of Education, ed. N.B. Henry, Part I (Chicago: the Society, 1955), citing Karl Marx, p. 190.
9. C. Wright Mills, *White Collar, the American Middle Classes* (New York: Oxford University Press, 1951), p. 237.
10. Robert S. Cohen, *op. cit.*, citing Karl Marx, p. 376.

CHAPTER 8

1. Genesis 2:2b.
2. Genesis 1:28.
3. Exodus 20:9.
4. Psalm 104:23.
5. Haggai 2:4b.
6. 1 Corinthians 9:6-12.

Notes

7. 2 Thessalonians 3:10b.
8. 2 Thessalonians 3:8.
9. 1 Thessalonians 4:11.
10. Ephesians 4:28.
11. Otto A. Piper, "The Meaning of Work," *Theology Today*, XIV, No. 2 (July 1957), p. 175.
12. Harvey Cox, *The Secular City* (New York: The Macmillan Company, 1965), citing Max Weber, p. 185.
13. Albert T. Rasmussen, *Christian Responsibility in Economic Life* (Philadelphia: The Westminster Press, 1965), p. 43.
14. Roland Bainton, *Here I Stand* (New York: Abingdon-Cokesbury, 1950), p. 233.
15. Thomas F. Green, *Work, Leisure, and the American Schools* (New York: Random House, 1968), p. 83.
16. *Ibid.*, p. 84.
17. Max Weber, *The Protestant Ethic and the Spirit of Capitalism* (New York: Charles Scribner's Sons, 1958), 292 pp.
18. Albert T. Rasmussen, *op. cit.*, p. 49.
19. Max Weber, *op. cit.*, p. 44.
20. Donald M. Royer, "Brethren Economic Ethic," *Brethren Life*, Vol. 3 (Summer, 1958), p. 59.
21. Quoted by Robert Lee, "Religion and Leisure," *Theology Today*, XIX, No. 1 (April 1962), p. 48.
22. Catherine Fennelly, editor, *New England Character and Characters*, Old Sturbridge Village Booklet Series (Sturbridge, Massachusetts, 1956), p. 22.
23. Albert T. Rasmussen, *op. cit.*, p. 57.
24. Max Weber, *op. cit.*, citing John Wesley, p. 175.
25. Thomas F. Green, *op. cit.*, pp. 103-111.
26. H. E. Brown, *Social Institutions* (New York: Prentice-Hall, 1942), citing Gus Dyer in a syndicated newspaper article (1939), p. 85.

CHAPTER 9

1. Franklin Luther Mott and Chester E. Jorgenson, *Benjamin Franklin* (New York: American Book Company, 1936), pp. 176, 196-198.
2. Rudyard Kipling, *Rudyard Kipling's Verse* (New York: Doubleday, 1934), p. 648.
3. Albert T. Rasmussen, *Christian Responsibility in Economic Life* (Philadelphia: The Westminster Press, 1965), p. 58.
4. Arnold J. Toynbee, "Why and How I Work," *Saturday Review* (April 5, 1969), p. 22.
5. Albert T. Rasmussen, *op. cit.*, p. 62.
6. *Ibid.*, p. 61.
7. Harvey Cox, *The Secular City* (New York: The Macmillan Company, 1965), p. 185.
8. Gordon J. Dahl, "Time, Work, and Leisure Today," *The Christian*

Century, Vol. 88 (February 10, 1971), p. 157.
  9. John M. Drescher, "Needed — Christian Doctrine of Work," *Gospel Herald*, Vol. LXIV, No. 34 (August 31, 1971), p. 713.
  10. *Ibid.*, p. 713.
  11. "The Job Blahs: Who Wants to Work?" *Newsweek*, Vol. LXXXI, No. 13 (March 26, 1973), pp. 79-89.
  12. Ernest Havemann, "The Emptiness of Too Much Leisure," *LIFE* Vol. 56 (February 14, 1964), p. 85.
  13. Harrison Brown, "Technology and Where We Are," *Technology, Human Values, and Leisure*, edited by Max Kaplan and Philip Bosserman (Nashville: Abingdom Press, 1971), p. 65.
  14. Editorial in *The Washington Post* (February 6, 1972).
  15. Albert T. Rasmussen, *op. cit.*, pp. 63-65.
  16. *Ibid.*, p. 66.
  17. Daniel R. Rusfeld, "Post-Post-Keynes: The Shattered Synthesis," *Saturday Review* (January 22, 1972), p. 39.
  18. John A. Kouwenhoven, "What's American About America?" *Harper's Magazine* (July 1956).
  19. Albert T. Rasmussen, *op. cit.*, pp. 69-71.
  20. *Ibid.*, pp. 76, 77.
  21. *Ibid.*, pp. 77, 78.
  22. *Ibid.*, pp. 84-88.

CHAPTER 10

  1. Ecclesiastes 2:24, 25.
  2. W. R. Forrester, *Christian Vocation* (New York: Charles Scribner's Sons, 1953), p. 23.
  3. Exodus 31:1-5.
  4. Virgil Vogt, *The Christian Calling*, Focal Pamphlet No. 6 (Scottdale, Pennsylvania: Mennonite Publishing House, 1961), 48 pp.
  5. Alan R. Richardson, *The Biblical Doctrine of Work* (Naperville, Illinois: Alan R. Richardson, Inc., 1958), Vol. I, *Ecumenical Biblical Studies*, pp. 35, 36.
  6. 1 Corinthians 7:20.
  7. Wade H. Boggs, Jr., *All Ye Who Labor* (Richmond, Virginia: John Knox Press, 1961), pp. 41, 42.
  8. Thomas F. Green, *Work, Leisure, and the American Schools* (New York: Random House, 1968), pp. 79-89.
  9. *Ibid.*, p. 79.
  10. *Ibid.*, p. 111.
  11. J. H. Oldman, *Work in Modern Society* (Richmond, Virginia: John Knox Press, 1950), pp. 57, 58.
  12. Luke 4:18.
  13. J. H. Oldham, *op. cit.*, pp. 50, 51.
  14. J. B. Phillips, *Letters to Young Churches* New York: The MacMillan Company, 1951), pp. 129-130.
  15. Ephesians 2:8-10.

16. Thomas F. Green, *op. cit.*, p. 79.
17. *Ibid.*, pp. 115-145.

CHAPTER 11

1. Joffre Dumazedier, "Leisure," *International Encyclopedia of the Social Studies,* IX (New York: Macmillan, 1968), p. 249.
2. Exodus 23:12.
3. Isaiah 58:13, 14.
4. Leviticus 25:20-22.
5. Matthew 14:13; 17:1; Mark 6:31; Luke 9:28.
6. Robert Lee, *Religion and Leisure in America* (New York: Abingdon Press, 1964), p. 132.
7. John Preston Dever, *Toward an Ethical Understanding of Leisure in a Technological Society,* unpublished ThD dissertation, Southern Baptist Theological Seminary, Louisville, Kentucky, 1968, p. 45.
8. Robert Lee, *op. cit.*, pp. 135-139.
9. John Preston Dever, *op. cit.*, p. 49.
10. Ibid., pp. 57, 58.
11. *Ibid.*, pp. 59-69.
12. Joffre Dumazedier, *op. cit.*, p. 249.
13. J. C. Wenger, "Place and Program of Recreation in the Home," paper read at the Recreation Study Conference, Elkhart, Indiana, November 29, 30, 1956, p. 1.
14. Melvin Gingerich, "Amusements," *The Mennonite Encyclopedia* (Scottdale, Pennsylvania: Mennonite Publishing House, 1955), p. 112.
15. Evan Oswald, "Recreational Trends in Our Brotherhood, Society, and Other Church Groups," paper read at the Recreation Study Conference, Elkhart, Indiana, November 29, 30, 1956, 16 pp.
16. *Ibid.*, p. 10.

CHAPTER 12

1. Josef Pieper, *Leisure, the Basis of Culture* (New York: Pantheon Books, 1964), 131 pp.
2. Robert Lee, *Religion and Leisure in America* (New York: Abingdon Press, 1964), 271 pp.
3. Rudolph F. Norden, *The Christian Encounters the New Leisure* (St. Louis: Concordia Publishing House, 1965), 105 pp.
4. Joseph H. Gates, "Work and Leisure," *The Asbury Seminarian,* Vol. XXV, No. 2 (April 1971), pp. 9-14.
5. Harvey Cox, *The Secular City* (New York: Macmillan, 1965), pp. 167-199.
6. Genesis 1:1, 31; 2:2, 3.
7. Exodus 31:17b.
8. Joseph H. Gates, *op. cit.*, p. 13.
9. Exodus 20:9-11.
10. Mark 2:27, 28.

11. Alan Richardson, *The Biblical Doctrine of Work* (London: SCM Press, 1952), p. 55.
12. Matthew 11:28, 29.
13. Robert Lee, *op. cit.*, pp. 55, 56.
14. Ephesians 5:16; Colossians 4:5.
15. Colossians 3:17.
16. Robert Lee, "Religion and Leisure in American Culture," *Theology Today*, Vol. XIX, No. 1 (April 1962), p. 57.
17. Robert Lee, *op. cit.*, p. 242.
18. *Ibid.*, citing Michel Quoist, "Lord, I Have Time" from *Prayers*, Sheed and Ward, Inc., Copyright, 1963, pp. 233, 234.
19. Thomas F. Green, *Work, Leisure, and the American School* (New York: Random House, 1968), p. 139.
20. H. Clair Amstutz, "The Fact and Significance of Leisure and the Need for Recreation," paper read at the Recreation Study Conference, Elkhart, Indiana, November 29, 30, 1956, p. 1.
21. Norman M. Lobsenz, *Is Anybody Happy?* (Garden City, New York: Doubleday & Co., 1962), pp. 76-78.
22. Harold D. Lehman, "Nonconformity in Recreational Activities," paper read at the Nonconformity Conference, Springdale Mennonite Church, Waynesboro, Virginia, November 18, 1955.
23. George F. Kneller, *Existentialism and Education* (New York: Philosophical Library, 1958), p. 131, citing Frederick Wilhelm Nietzsche, *On the Future of Our Educational Institutions* (New York: Macmillan Company, 1924), pp. 95, 96.
24. H. Clair Amstutz, *op. cit.*, p. 5.
25. Harvey Cox, *op. cit.*, p. 189.
26. Leo Perlis, "Implications for Labor Unionism," *Technology, Human Values, and Leisure*, edited by Max Kaplan and Philip Bosserman (New York: Abingdon Press, 1971), p. 101.
27. Harvey Cox, *op. cit.*, pp. 125-148.
28. M. H. and E. S. Neumeyer, *Leisure and Recreation*, 3rd edition (New York: Ronald Press, 1958), p. 1.
29. 1 Timothy 4:7, 8, Weymouth.
30. 1 Corinthians 6:19, 20.
31. Thomas F. Green, *op. cit.*, pp. 138-140.
32. H. Clair Amstutz, *op. cit.*, p. 5.
33. William P. H. Stevens, Jr., *Are We Ready for Leisure?* (New York: Friendship Press, 1966), pp. 49-57.
34. Josef Pieper, *op. cit.*, p. 44.
35. *Ibid.*, pp. 44-49.
36. Max Kaplan, *Leisure in America* (New York: Wiley, 1960), p. 291.
37. Harvey Cox, *The Feast of Fools* (Cambridge, Massachusetts: Harvard University Press, 1969), 204 pp.
38. Harvey Cox, "In Praise of Festivity," *Saturday Review*, Vol. 52 (October 25, 1969), p. 25.
39. Proverbs 8:22, 23, 30, 31.

Notes

40. Luke 10:40-42.
41. Hebrews 4:8-11a.

CHAPTER 13

1. Gordon J. Dahl, *Work, Play, and Worship in a Leisure-Oriented Society* (Minneapolis: Augsburg Publishing House, 1972), p. 12.
2. "Leisure Boom," *U.S. News and World Report*, LXXII, No. 16 (April 17, 1972), pp. 42-45.
3. Robin W. Doughty and Michael Morrison, "The Three-Day American Pleasure Trip," *Natural History*, LXXXI, No. 6 (June 1972), pp. 22, 23.
4. Gordon J. Dahl, *op. cit.*, p. 102.
5. John Muir, cited by Donald C. Peattie, "Everybody Needs Beauty," *Reader's Digest*, Vol. 55, No. 329 (September 1949), p. 86.
6. James F. Murphy, "The Counter Culture of Leisure," *Parks and Recreation*, VII, No. 2 (February 1972), p. 34.
7. Gordon J. Dahl, *op. cit.*, p. 90.
8. *Ibid.*, pp. 78-82.
9. *Ibid.*, pp. 82-87.
10. *Ibid.*, p. 83.
11. *Ibid.*, pp. 89, 90.
12. 1 Peter 2:9.
13. Galatians 4:19.
14. Rudolph Norden, *The Christian Encounters the New Leisure* (St. Louis: Concordia, 1965), p. 90.
15. See the Mennonite Position Statement on "Recreation," *The Story and Witness of the Christian Way*, edited by Ernest D. Martin (Scottdale, Pennsylvania: Mennonite Publishing House, 1971), pp. 88-90.

CHAPTER 14

1. J. C. Hoekendijk, *The Church Inside Out* (Philadelphia: Westminster Press, 1966), p. 82.
2. Arnold Cressman, "A Philosophy of Christian Education for the Congregation," unpublished manuscript prepared for the Philosophy of Christian Education Study Committee, June 4-7, 1968, p. 90.
3. William P. H. Stevens, Jr., *Are We Ready for Leisure?* (New York: Friendship Press, 1966), p. 55.
4. Harvey Cox, "In Praise of Festivity,"*Saturday Review*, Vol. LII, No. 43 (October 25, 1969), p. 27.
5. Josef Pieper, *Leisure, the Basis of Culture* (New York: Pantheon Books, 1964), p. 44.
6. *Ibid.*, p. 49.
7. Charles K. Brightbill, *Man and Leisure* (Englewood Cliffs, New Jersey: Prentice-Hall, 1961), pp. 96-101.
8. Psalm 46:10a.
9. John Preston Dever, *Toward an Ethical Understanding of Leisure in a Technological Society*, unpublished ThD dissertation, Southern Baptist Theological Seminary, Louisville, Kentucky, 1968, p. 156.

The Conrad Grebel Lectures

The Conrad Grebel Lectureship was set up in 1950 for the purpose of making possible an annual study by a Mennonite scholar of some topic of interest and value to the Mennonite Church and to other Christian people. It is administered by the Conrad Grebel Lectureship Committee appointed by and responsible to the Mennonite Board of Education. The committee appoints the lecturers, approves their subjects, counsels them during their studies, and arranges for the delivery of the lectures at one or more places.

The lectureship is financed by donors who contribute annually $500 each.

Conrad Grebel was an influential leader in the sixteenth-century Swiss Anabaptist movement and is honored as one of the founders of the Mennonite Church.

The lectures are published by Herald Press, Scottdale, Pa. 15683, as soon as feasible after the delivery of the lectures. The date of publication by Herald Press is indicated by parenthesis.

Lectures thus far delivered are as follows:

1952 — Foundations of Christian Education, by Paul Mininger.

The Conrad Grebel Lectures

1953 — The Challenge of Christian Stewardship (1955), by Milo Kauffman.
1954 — The Way of the Cross in Human Relations (1958), by Guy F. Hershberger.
1955 — The Alpha and the Omega (1955), by Paul Erb.
1956 — The Nurture and Evangelism of Children (1959), by Gideon G. Yoder.
1957 — The Holy Spirit and the Holy Life (1959), by Chester K. Lehman.
1959 — The Church Apostolic (1960), by J. D. Graber.
1960 — These Are My People (1962), by Harold S. Bender.
1963 — Servant of God's Servants (1964), by Paul M. Miller.
1964 — The Resurrected Life (1965), by John R. Mumaw.
1965 — Creating Christian Personality (1966), by A. Don Augsburger.
1966 — God's Word Written (1966), by J. C. Wenger.
1967 — The Christian and Revolution (1968), by Melvin Gingerich.
1968-1969 — The Discerning Community — Church Renewal, by J. Lawrence Burkholder.
1970 — Woman Liberated (1971), by Lois Gunden Clemens.
1973 — In Praise of Leisure (1974), by Harold D. Lehman.

Index of Persons

Adler, Mortimer, 81
Amstutz, H. Clair, 140, 149
Aristotle, 27
Aquinas, Thomas, 87, 127

Bainton, Roland, 89
Bellman, Richard, 65
Boggs, Wade H., Jr., 113
Brightbill, Charles, 58, 183
Brunner, Emil, 144
Burck, Gilbert, 61

Cabot, Richard C., 33
Calvin, John, 88-90, 127
Carnegie, Andrew, 99
Clark, Francis L., 78
Cohen, Robert S., 82
Conwell, Russell, 99
Cox, Harvey, 134, 145, 146, 151, 181
Cressman, Arnold, 177

Dahl, Gordon J., 100, 157, 164, 165
de Grazia, Sebastian, 27, 36, 60, 66, 80
Desmond, Thomas G., 133
Dever, John Preston, 126, 183
Dostoevski, Fyodor, 77

Drescher, John, 101
Dumazedier, Joffre, 29, 61, 129

Edison, Thomas, 29
Emerson, Ralph W., 23

Forrester, W. R., 112
Franklin, Benjamin, 97, 98, 104
Frisch, Max, 64
Fromm, Eric, 59
Frost, Robert, 174

Garfield, James A., 21
Gates, Joseph H., 134, 135
Gingerich, Melvin, 131
Godby, Geoffrey, 48
Green, Thomas F., 89, 115, 116

Haveman, Ernest, 70
Heckscher, August, 38, 60
Hoekendijk, J. C., 175
Huizinga, Johan, 32, 151
Hutchins, Robert, 47

Kahn, Herman, 51
Kaplan, Max, 22, 25, 30, 50, 51, 54
Kerr, Walter, 28

Index

Kipling, Rudyard, 98
Kouwenhoven, John A., 106

Lee, Robert, 29, 36, 60, 126, 134, 136, 168
Lincoln, Abraham, 104
Linder, Staffan B., 23, 24
Luther, John, 123
Luther, Martin, 88-90, 127, 152
Lynes, Russell, 56

MacIver, Robert, 72
Mann, Horace, 97
Marx, Karl, 82
Mills, C. Wright, 22, 82
Muir, John, 162
Murphy, James F., 164

Nader, Ralph, 108
Nash, Jay B., 38-42
Neumeyer, M. H. and E. S., 147
New, A. L., 63
Nietzsche, Frederick, 143
Nordon, Rudolf F., 134, 167

Oates, Wayne E., 77
Oswald, Evan, 131, 132

Parker, Sanford S., 64
Perlis, Leo, 146
Pieper, Josef, 29, 133, 150, 182, 183

Piper, Otto, 87
Plato, 151
Post, Lindsay, 17

Quoist, Michel, 139

Rasmussen, Albert T., 88, 93, 99, 100, 103, 109, 110
Reich, Charles, 63, 68, 72
Richardson, Alan, 113
Royer, Donald, 91
Russell, Bertrand, 55, 71

Saunders, Dero A., 64
Schlesinger, Arthur, Jr., 69
Shakespeare, William, 152
Sidney, Algernon, 104
Socrates, 25
Spencer, Herbert, 99
Stevens, William, Jr., 150
Sutton, Francis X., 99

Tournier, Paul, 111
Toynbee, Arnold J., 98

Vogt, Virgil, 113

Weber, Max, 88, 90, 91
Wenger, J. C., 130
Wesley, John, 85, 95
Wiener, Anthony J., 51

Index of Subjects

Aquinas, St. Thomas
  and leisure, 127
  and work, 87
Amusements, 42, 131, 132

Blue-collar worker, 67-73
Boredom and leisure, 42, 63-65, 140
Brethren, Church of the, 91
Business
  activism, 106
  competition, 107
  consumer sovereignty, 108
  creed, 99, 100
  individualism, 103
  productivity, 105
  progress and optimism, 106
  self-interest, 108
  self-reliance, 104

Calvin, John

and leisure, 127
and work, 88-90
Campus Crusade, 168
Capitalism, 90
Celebration and leisure, 125, 150, 151, 164, 181, 182
Choice and leisure, 31, 38, 147, 148, 170
Christ
   and rest, 124, 125, 136, 152
   and work, 36, 117
   lordship of, 137
Christian church and leisure, 125, 166-173
Christian service, 172, 173
Congregation and leisure, 175-182
Conservation, 162
Consumer economy, 23, 57-59
Conveniences, household, 53
Counterculture and leisure, 164-166
Creation model for leisure, 134-136
Cybernation, 49, 50, 52, 63

Ethics of leisure, 134-153, 158-160, 164-166

Gross national product, 105

Holidays and holy days, 51, 125-129
Homemaking, 83, 84

Industrial Revolution, 153
Inter-Varsity Christian Fellowship, 168

Jesus (see Christ)
Job (or jobs)
   and work, 115, 116
   enrichment, 102, 103
   moonlighting, 60
Job-residence separation, 54, 62

Leisure
   advance of, 47-55
   age of, 18
   an attitude or spirit, 29, 148-150
   and celebration, 125, 150, 151, 164, 181, 182
   and choice, 38, 147, 148
   and counterculture, 164-166
   and freedom, 28, 56
   and the church, 125, 166-182
   and time, 36
   and work, 22, 26, 77-79, 119, 120
   and worship, 182-184
   as activity, 27, 28
   as privilege of upper class, 21, 27
   causes of leisure potential, 49-55
   challenges of, 157-166
   definitions for, 25-30
   ethics of, 134-153, 164-166
   fact and myth, 18
   Greek and Roman, 27, 40
   harried leisure, 23, 59, 60
   New Testament views, 125, 135, 136
   Old Testament views, 124, 135
   risks of, 40, 44
   theological assumptions, 134-153
   values of, 21
Leisure consumption, 23, 57-59, 160, 161, 170
Leisure guidance, 169-172
Leisure Witness Study Committee, 134
Luther's views
   on leisure, 127, 152
   on work, 88-90

Mennonites, 91, 129-132, 168
Middle Ages, 87, 126
Moonlighting, 60

National Council of Churches, 134, 168
National Park Service, 161, 162
Natural environment, 1 , 162
New Leisure, 157-166
New Testament views
   on leisure, 125, 135, 136
   on work, 86
Old Testament views
   on leisure, 124, 135
   on work, 85

Index

Participation
  active, 43
  creative, 43
  emotional, 42
  passive, 42, 64
Play
  a function of leisure, 31-33
  children's play, 31
Post-industrial society, 65, 73, 74
Professional workers, 66-74
Protestant work ethic, 90-92, 100-102, 115, 153, 158
Puritan work ethic, 59, 92-94, 128

Quakers, 91

Recreation
  an accepted use of leisure, 30
  as re-creation, 136
  passive recreation, 42, 64, 69, 70
  types of, 141
Recreation Study Committee, 168
Rest, as leisure, 125, 135, 151, 152
Retirement, 50, 53, 163, 181

Stewardship and leisure, 170

Technology, 33
Time
  and leisure, 36, 138, 139
  and work, 36
  commuting time loss, 62
  free time, 26, 37, 61
  subsistence time, 37
  use of God's gift of time, 138, 139
  work-related time, 37

Time, views of
  cyclical, 34
  linear, 35
  quantitative, 35
Transportation and leisure, 54

Vacation time, 50, 51, 163
Vocation, Christian, 88-90, 112-115, 144-148
Voluntary service, 173, 179

Work
  a Christian's work, 116-119
  and Christian vocation, 112-115
  and job, 115, 116
  and leisure, 22, 27, 77, 119
  and time, 36
  as a boring grind, 22
  benefits of, 79-84, 94-96
  Christian ethic of, 101, 111-119
  definitions for, 33, 34, 79-84
  early Christian church views, 86, 87
  labor and toil, 79
  meanings of, 79-84
  Medieval church views, 87
  New Testament views, 86
  Old Testament views, 85
  Protestant ethic, 88-92, 100-102, 115, 153, 158
  Puritan ethic, 59, 92-94, 128
  work ethic, 94-110, 111, 158-160
  work ethic criticized, 100-110
  work-residence separation, 54
Worship and leisure, 182-184

The Author

Harold D. Lehman's leisure activities include reading, stamp-collecting, jogging, and tennis. He has directed summer camping programs in Pennsylvania at Tel-Hai Camp and at Laurelville Mennonite Church Center. He is on the executive board of Mennonite Camping Association.

For many years, Lehman was physical education director at Eastern Mennonite College, Harrisonburg, Virginia, and later served as college registrar. From 1957-1962 he was principal of Eastern Mennonite High School in the same community.

Lehman has participated in regional and churchwide study conferences and in the preparation of positive statements on recreation by his denomination.

Lehman has been professor of education at Madison College, Harrisonburg, Virginia, since 1967. He received a BS degree from Madison College, an MEd degree from Pennsylvania State University, and EdD degree from University of Virginia.

He is currently chairman of Rockingham County Chapter of the American Red Cross and of the Commission on Congregational Education and Literature of the Mennonite Church.